W9-AMO-840

Praise for Raja Shehadeh

Going Home

"*Going Home* cements the author's reputation as the best-known Palestinian writing in English."

—Ian Black, *The Guardian*

"*Going Home* is about searching for the meaning of 'home' when living in a city under occupation. . . . In this book, the bonds that bind Palestinians to the land are exposed. Personal and political, human and geographical histories are beautifully intertwined and preserved."

—Claire Kohda Hazelton, *The Spectator*

"Luminously clear-sighted. . . . By turns lyrical, witty and shrewd, Shehadeh is an excellent walking companion."

—Matt Rowland Hill, *Prospect*

"An insightful, illuminating book"

—Paddy Kehoe, *RTÉ*

Where the Line Is Drawn

"No one else writes about Palestinian life under military occupation with such stubborn humanity, melancholy, and fragile grace. . . . One feels the loss in every paragraph Shehadeh writes, but also the inescapable beauty that remains, which both softens and deepens the rage."

—Ben Ehrenreich, *The Guardian*

"Writing has allowed Shehadeh to continue crossing into these territories, even as they become increasingly off-limits to him. His books are maps, painstakingly pieced together, of regions lost to senseless division, to bad choices, and to lies."

—Ursula Lindsey, *The Nation*

"Remarkable and hopeful . . . a deeply honest and intense memoir."

—Gal Beckerman, *The New York Times Book Review*

"Shehadeh describes with courage and grace the internal struggle to remain fair."

—*The New Yorker*

"A beautifully impressionistic exploration of shared cultural understanding despite the narrowing of borders."

—*Kirkus Reviews*

"Shehadeh's incisive, lyrical memoir cuts to the core of a complex cultural identity."

—*Financial Times*

"The question of how and if friendships can survive across political divides is a resonant one, and I can think of no one better than Raja Shehadeh to treat it with the wisdom, toughness and humanity that it deserves."

—Kamila Shamsie

"Raja Shehadeh's *Where the Line Is Drawn* is a courageous and timely meditation on the fragility of friendship in dark times, illuminating how affiliation and love—without pretence or concealment, in defiance of occupation and

estrangement—can have a profound political power. I hope
many people will read and dwell on this unforgettable book."

—Madeleine Thien

"While I was in Ramallah, I met the Palestinian writer Raja
Shehadeh, whose work I did not previously know. His books—
including *Strangers in the House* and *When the Birds Stopped
Singing*—were a discovery: he is a great inquiring spirit with a
tone that is vivid, ironic, melancholy, and wise."

—Colm Tóibín

"In the dark agony of the Palestine-Israel conflict, Raja Shehadeh
offers a rare gift: a lucid, honest, unsparing voice. His humanity
and wisdom are invaluable. *Where the Line Is Drawn* powerfully
records many testing aspects of Shehadeh's life under Israeli
occupation, but at its heart is his long-lived friendship with a
fellow intellectual and seeker, Jewish and Israeli. In their bond
lies reason for hope. . . . It's a beautiful book."

—Claire Messud

"The weight of oppression, as Raja Shehadeh calls it, bears
down on every page of this delicate, thoughtful memoir of
Palestinian life under Israeli occupation."

—Fatima Bhutto

Palestinian Walks

"A work of passionate polemic, journeying, history, and autobi-
ography, this highly original consideration of the Palestinian-
Israeli issue is structured around a series of vigorous, attentive
hikes through the occupied territories. . . . Ranks with Sari
Nusseibeh's memoir, *Once Upon a Country*."

—*The New Yorker*

"Few Palestinians have opened their minds and their hearts with such frankness."

—*The New York Times*

"This beautiful book is not just a guide to the Palestinian present; it is an Israeli album of what is taking place in a faraway land: Palestine."

—*Haaretz*

"Raja Shehadeh's *Palestinian Walks* provides a rare historical insight into the tragic changes taking place in Palestine."

—Jimmy Carter

"A thoughtful meditation on Palestine, the land and the peoples who claim it."

—Mahmood Mamdani

"This constantly surprising book modestly describes walking along certain paths which have touched the lived lives of two millennia. . . . His confessions often encounter a perennial wisdom, and what he is talking about and walking across is one of the nodal points of the world's present crisis. I strongly suggest you walk with him."

—John Berger

"This exquisitely written book records a sensitive Palestinian writer's love for the landscape of his country, over which he has hiked for many years. It reflects not only the intense beauty of that landscape, but also some of the terrible dangers that threaten it and its occupants."

—Rashid Khalidi

GOING HOME

GOING HOME

A Walk Through Fifty Years of Occupation

RAJA SHEHADEH

NEW YORK
LONDON

Requests for permission to reproduce selections from this book should
be made through our website: https://thenewpress.com/contact.

Originally published in Great Britain by Profile Books Ltd
Published in the United States by The New Press, New York, 2020
Distributed by Two Rivers Distribution

ISBN 978-1-62097-577-0 (hc)
ISBN 978-1-62097-578-7 (ebook)
CIP data is available

The New Press publishes books that promote and enrich public
discussion and understanding of the issues vital to our democracy
and to a more equitable world. These books are made possible by
the enthusiasm of our readers; the support of a committed group of
donors, large and small; the collaboration of our many partners in the
independent media and the not-for-profit sector; booksellers, who often
hand-sell New Press books; librarians; and above all by our authors.

www.thenewpress.com

This book was set in Dante

Printed in the United States of America

2   4   6   8   10   9   7   5   3   1

To Ingmar Bergman, whose film *Wild Strawberries*
was an inspiration for this book

Perhaps home is not a place but simply
an irrevocable condition.

James Baldwin, *Giovanni's Room*

A Note to the Reader

Palestinian Walks, published in 2007, is my account of walking in the Palestinian hills and reflecting on my work and life under occupation. The walks described there took place over a twenty-seven-year period. In this book I describe a walk that I took in the course of one day – the fiftieth anniversary of the occupation – in Ramallah, the city of my birth, trying to come to terms with the political defeats, frustrations and failures that I have witnessed over the years of occupation and resistance, as well as the changes in the city where I live. I also reflect on ageing as I visit and remember the places, people and events in my life. All this, to be able to arrive home and, in the words of Derek Walcott, look in the mirror, greet the face reflected and 'smile at the other's welcome'.

One

It must already be eight, I think, as I listen to the national anthem blasting out of St George's School near my house in Ramallah. I am standing at the bathroom sink, manoeuvring the shaving blade around the deep folds in my face that have formed over the last few years. Next I comb the remaining strands of hair – still black – left on my balding head with my old brush. My once-abundant hair seems to have made its way south to my nose. There, bursting from my nostrils, I can see plenty that need clipping. How furious my father used to be when I borrowed his scissors to cut my newly emerging moustache and failed to put them back where he could find them. How could I have known then that he needed them for this older man's purpose? As I bring the scissors up to my nose, I examine the brown liver spots on my hands and notice that there are more of them on my temples. I wonder how long they've been there. Next I study the worryingly persistent red sun patch on my hand. Had I been closer to my father as he was getting on in years, I could have learned about these changes that our bodies go through as they age and been better prepared for what was to come.

After finishing my grooming I look in the mirror again. It's all there in front of me: the bags under my eyes, the furrowed forehead, the corners of my mouth that used to be mobile but have now descended into a permanently sad expression.

Disappointment is written all over my face, expressing the real experiences and pains I have struggled through. I no longer have that silly smirk, that effacing, distant and unreal expression I wore most of the time. The face I see before me has been broken down and reassembled. It's the confirmation of my holding fast, of not escaping or avoiding, of being baptised by fire. It expresses what I have felt and tells all without hiding anything. But things are better this way.

I try to convince myself that I'm as old as my face, which is not at all how I feel. Mine is already the face of an older man, sombre and serious, with thin lips and wrinkles that bring my expression so much closer to that of my father. My ears, which were always large, seem to have increased in size. My black eyes, with long eyelashes, are no longer radiant. It used to be that my whole being spoke through my sparkling eyes. Now the look is inward. I have aged with the years and with the occupation. Today, 5 June 2017, marks its fiftieth anniversary.

With every year I come to resemble my father more and more. I first became aware of our striking likeness a few years back, during a particularly tense time. I remember entering the barber shop where I have had my hair cut since I was five and where my father had also been a customer. Looking in the mirror as I entered, I was struck by what I saw: mine was the face of an anxious man holding himself together, wearing a fur karakul hat, the same hat my father used to wear, and a thick Harris tweed jacket with wide shoulder pads to add bulk. Yet inside this heavy garment I was small. And of course I thought of my father. When he was getting on he would have a similar look, holding himself awkwardly, thinking of himself as a younger man and straining to achieve the look, but with the tension showing regardless.

As my father advanced in years he seemed to gain energy and act more youthful. My mother often wondered where he got this energy from and suspected it was the large number of vitamin pills he was taking, if they were indeed vitamins. I thought then that this was a premonition of how I would look in later life, not occasionally but permanently, old and uncomfortable, yet straining to look happy – an assumed air of well-being that would deceive no one.

These days thoughts of my father are with me more often. For a long time, as I was growing up, he was like a mystery that I wanted to explore. The ailments of his ageing body and his mood swings were never discussed, perhaps because he was too proud or too anxious about growing old, so I did not know how he dealt with them. His sacrosanct law office was another mystery. I almost held my breath when I visited. His politics, his relationship with my mother, his death – all remain unresolved in my mind. But perhaps most mysterious of all was his life in Jaffa, which I wanted to emulate but couldn't, much as I tried when I lived in Beirut and London. Jaffa, the metropolis, remains the place of my imaginings where he lived his fantasy life by the sea, in a prosperous and vibrant city. It will always have that special resonance for me, but it's here in Ramallah where I find my parents, myself and my life scattered around in the various houses in which I've lived and written my books.

Every morning when I look in the mirror a serious face stares back. I try to remember that the face I have imprinted on my mind is not the face others see. I know I have another side to me, but who else would know it from looking at me? Where and when did these markers of age appear? How much manipulation and control do we have over how we look? Does our face always betray us? Is the relaxed face of a child – that time of our life when we seem to live most in the present – the real face, the real mirror of who we are? Perhaps there is little I can do to conceal anything. They say we get the face we deserve, but is that really true? It strikes me now that each memoir I've written is but another interpretation of my life. So maybe the way my face has matured is just another sort of memoir, one that is imprinted and that I am not in control of; maybe this one is the most honest.

After the Oslo Accords were signed between Israel and the PLO in the mid-1990s my dentist told me that I was grinding my teeth and putting pressure on my gums. And so I was. Perhaps this was distorting my face. Are those who undergo Botox treatment removing the markers of ageing, returning their face to its original true expression, or are they committing a further distortion?

As I get dressed I flex my fingers to check they're still pliable. In 2004, rushing to a session at the International Court of Justice in The Hague on the legality of the wall that Israel was building, I stumbled on the stairs and broke my little finger. The doctor who treated me then said it was likely to become arthritic. I'm pleased to find that it is still not painful.

Now I can hear the second bell from the nearby school, summoning students to their classrooms. It so happens that every house I've lived in has had a school next to it. I didn't plan it that way. When we moved to our present home I thought this was going to be an exception, but soon St George's School was built close by, preserving the pattern. Then, a short while later, a nursery was opened right across the street with the bombastic name Kids Academy. After the school bell I hear the birds singing. Loudest of all is the bulbul, which often wakes us in the morning.

My parents, who were well off, never built their own house.

In the beginning this was because they thought they would soon be returning to Jaffa, to the home they were forced to leave in 1948. Then, in the late 1950s, my father had an architect prepare plans for a palatial home which would be the house of his dreams, with large rooms for sumptuous social gatherings and parties. But this was not to my mother's liking. All she saw was what hard work it would take to maintain such a house and cater for large numbers of guests. They never agreed, and the plans for the new house remained mere ink on paper.

For a long time I too resolved not to build a house of my own for fear of getting too attached to it and then losing it in this unsettled land of ours, ending up spending the rest of my life lamenting its loss, as happened to my parents. It was only after the Oslo Accords and the confusion and chaos that came in their wake that I decided I needed a place to which I could retire at the end of the day, a place of order and tranquillity. When the deal was signed in 1995, I had an intimation of what Ramallah would be like. I had seen how crowded Nazareth, the only Palestinian city in Israel, had grown. It was perhaps this scary view of the future of this land – Arab enclaves in the midst of sprawling Israeli settlements – that started me thinking about building my own house.

But what clinched it and made me take the final plunge was that one day in 1992, after my marriage to Penny, I returned home from work and saw a group of people assembled in front of the main door of the building in which I had rented a flat. I enquired what was going on and was told that these people had come to intervene between the landlord and one of the ground-floor tenants.

The landlord, Abu Ameen, seemed in a perpetual muddle, with sweat streaming down his face, like a drowning man who feels the end is nigh and wants to make the most of the time left. He had been a pedlar in the US and had for a long

time breathed heavily from what he said was fabric fluff as
he auctioned clothes. Perhaps the truth was that he sold old
clothes and wanted to upgrade his status by claiming to be an
auctioneer.

His campaigns against the tenants in his building began when
he blocked the front door of the downstairs tenants without
asking permission, forcing them to enter their flat through a
back door. This was done in stealth. When the guileless wife
tried to open the door and it wouldn't budge, she told me she
thought one of the children had sealed it with chewing gum.
She tried pushing with all her might, but realised there was a
wall of concrete behind it. Abu Ameen had once built a wall
to block their view of his garden and he had also cemented
the chimneys so that another neighbour couldn't use a wood
stove. Such actions caused ridiculous squabbles, with each side
bringing friends to bolster their positions. This was a time when
there were no functioning police or courts of law. One's protection depended on how many thugs one could rally to one's side.
That afternoon there was a lot of screaming and mayhem. I
realised then that we were not going to be spared such incidents
and that should my rights in my rented flat be trampled on I
would be unable to muster support. At that moment I decided
to take the plunge and build a house for myself and Penny, so
we would not have to endure daily chaos whenever I left my flat
to go to work and more chaos when I returned.

Abu Ameen, our eccentric landlord, had made his money in the
US and returned home to Ramallah to retire, full of romantic
fantasies about living a simple life close to nature. He spent
most of his time designing the strangest garden, in which he
aspired to grow only the wild shrubs and herbs that grew in the
hills behind his house. But he wasn't satisfied by following the
existing design of the large plot of land that extended from his

building all the way down to the street. He wanted to expose the bedrock and work up from there. To realise his odd schemes, he employed a fleet of young, destitute men who were treated like slaves, along with a bewildered donkey, to carry heavy loads of rocks and plants brought from the hills to his garden. The large slabs of rock that he exposed he used to mark pathways leading to the different levels of the garden, which soon began to look like no other. Some slabs he propped up and used as borders for new beds, which he filled with soil before planting the medley of shrubs and herbs, some spiky evergreens, others herbaceous, all very close together. He used other slabs to hold the soil around the ancient furrowed trunks of the olive trees that had been on the land. Periodically he would light a fire in the centre of each of these trees. He had been told by some knowledgeable American farmer that the olive trees in Palestine are afflicted by a certain virus that reduces their productivity and the only way to get rid of it is to light a fire in the tree. Miraculously, only one tree burned to the core; the others somehow survived, so resilient are olive trees.

On the top part of the garden he created a seating area with a table and benches, all made using the rocks he had excavated. He once took me on a tour of this strange garden and, after we had walked down pathways shaded by canopies of all sorts of trees and pushed against a mishmash of shrubs and herbs, I found myself entirely bewildered, unable to see beyond the garden or be seen by anyone on the street or in the building. I thought this must have been precisely the atmosphere he wanted to create, a world of his own design in which he could lose himself.

Now the building, along with the garden, has been sold by his heirs. The new owner transformed the garden into a restaurant café called Al Reef (the countryside), which has been highly successful.

Our decision to build our own house, where we would never have to worry about the antics of an obsessive landlord, turned out to be one of the best decisions we ever took. Land prices had not yet risen astronomically, as they have since. At first we planned to build on land we owned right across from the house where I was born and had lived until I was sixteen. But my brother, Samer, advised against it, and he was right. The area is now bustling and noisy, and the much-cherished view of the Ramallah hills, reaching all the way to the west, which had been the main attraction of the land, has been blocked by new buildings. Instead, we found a good-sized plot at the edge of town in the Tireh quarter (so called because it is one of the highest and windiest parts of town) on a quiet street north of the city and began planning. We decided that the house would be built around an inner courtyard, so the view wouldn't be blocked by any future construction work near the house. As it was going up, we would walk to the site in the afternoon and enjoy seeing the house materialise stone by stone. It is traditional to place in the foundations some precious metal as an omen of future prosperity; instead we decided to write on a parchment how we wished our life in the house to be lived, rolled it up and inserted it into a pipe, which we buried. Will anyone read what we wrote at some future time? I very much doubt it. If this should happen, I wonder what they will think of us. But we didn't mean it for posterity. The foundations of our house with the buried script of hopes must by now have become enmeshed within the roots of the lemon tree we planted in the middle of the courtyard. Or perhaps with those of the three olive trees in the backyard that are sure to outlive us. Everything else will die except those resilient trees. Most likely, the text of our aspirations has returned to nature, as our bodies will some day.

In the bedroom we had built a walk-in wardrobe. As I stood

there trying to decide what to put on, I was aware of the significance of this day. Past anniversaries of the occupation used to arouse strong feelings in me and I would try to ward them off by taking a long walk in the hills. It used to be possible to leave the city behind me. This was preferable to staying at home and brooding. Today I will walk to the office, taking my time. My first meeting is not until one-thirty this afternoon. Perhaps more will be happening than I expect.

I stood in front of the shirts and coats from different periods of my life, among which is a charcoal-grey pullover knitted by my grandmother which I haven't worn for years but cannot part with. My wardrobe is a museum spanning decades. Because I've remained the same size and haven't gained weight for years, I can still wear many garments, yet I rarely do. I am tempted to believe that, like my city, my wardrobe – the various shirts, suits, hats or ties – is a repository of what I've tried to be. Some of my father's clothes are still here. They are so much him that my mother could not throw them away. She gave them to me, hoping that I would wear them, though I could never bring myself to. I'm a hoarder and have a hard time throwing away any possession – especially clothes that remind me of other periods of my life.

When I walk in, I am bewildered by the choice I have, but I always end up going for my favourite clothes, which I keep even after they get holes in them. Clothes are like houses, objects we cover ourselves with and often dwell in so as to create an impression for others and not just for the comfort they provide. My different lives are represented by the different clothes I have worn, as by the homes located in different parts of the city where I have lived. To this day I have my writerly clothes and my lawyerly ones, some from when I started my career thirty-seven years ago – shirts, belts, trousers and jackets.

Like our bodies, our houses and our clothing are but sparks

of our existence, our self, which we inhabit for a while and make our own. Then we leave them and the connection is severed. Clothes wear out and houses are sold to other owners or fall into ruin, and the city continues as if we were never there. Until the city itself ceases to exist, whether through war or natural disasters, and then it is as though it never ever was.

Barring some political or natural calamity, Penny and I hope to spend the rest of our days in this house. And yet, despite this long-standing attachment, I continue to be troubled by a recurring dream in which, for what feels to be an agonisingly long time, I search for but cannot find my home. For someone who has lived the majority of his life in the same small city, who owns a property in it, to feel in my subconscious that I'm bereft of a home is a strange affliction. This was what I was thinking that morning, a little after nine, when I prepared to leave my house, dressed in a clean, well-ironed, black-and-white-striped shirt and dark trousers (my lawyerly clothes today), to walk to my law office in the centre of town.

Two

The morning sun was shining through the eastern window, lighting up the sitting room. This is the best time of day. I could hear Penny settling down with a book on the sofa by the window, her mug of coffee next to her, listening to music while the sun streaked in, and I wondered, why am I leaving?

As I was walking to the door, I glanced at the Byzantine jar that we bought from an antiques shop in Jerusalem as a present for our new house. It was next to the piano, resting in a black metal stand. For the first three years after we moved in, the jar stood on the floor. Then, nineteen years ago, when I was at home working one day, the doorbell rang and I found the principal of the Lutheran Vocational Training School in Jerusalem standing at the door. A young man with highly pronounced muscles, he was carrying a number of metal stands that I had ordered a month earlier for various flowerpots and one for the jar. He told me that he had decided to deliver them in person to make sure they were to my liking. I thanked him, paid and took them inside. Choosing one I thought would be the right size, I carefully lifted the ancient jar and gingerly placed it on the

stand. It didn't fit: the ring was too small; the jar needed a wider one. I chose another stand that I thought would be perfect and slowly slid the jar in. It seemed the right size, but once I let go the jar passed right through my fingers and broke into many pieces. Nineteen years later I can still feel that sinking feeling as this centuries-old prized possession slipped down and shattered. I looked mournfully at the pieces of the once-beautiful jar now scattered on the floor and immediately started blaming myself for not taking more care in handling this piece of pottery that had been in use for a long time before it came to be displayed in our house. What had I done? How could I not have known that I should have used more care? My mind turned to how to put it back together again. I ran to the kitchen to get a broom and swept every single shard into a plastic bag. The evidence was removed, yet the jar was gone. Unwilling to accept this, I decided I must reassemble it. As I stood back and looked at the empty metal holder that was supposed to enhance the appeal of the jar but had led only to its demise, I thought how like Palestine was this precious old jar, once whole and lovely, now reduced to shards.

When Penny got home I told her what had happened and assured her that I would put the jar back together. Kindly, she resisted expressing doubts, but she made it clear that she thought I had better accept the loss of that lovely historic jar.

A year passed. And another. Penny was getting tired of having a pottery-shard-filled plastic bag in our pantry and yet I insisted that some day I would reassemble the jar. Then, with the end of the century approaching, I thought it would be a bad omen to start the new one with a broken jar on my conscience. I gave myself ample time and began on 1 December 1999. I spread the shards on my desk and got to work. The most difficult section was the base, but as soon as that was accomplished the sides proved easier to fit together. I kept at it and before the century ended I had glued the jar back together. There is a Japanese art of fixing broken pottery called *kintsugi*. I didn't exactly follow that practice, where the shards are fixed with a special lacquer dusted with powdered gold; instead I used ordinary slow-drying glue. In Japan these repaired ceramic pieces are believed to be more valuable than unbroken ones.

My jar is now whole again. You can see the individual pieces when light shines through the holes which I failed to fill, but you can appreciate the effort of rebuilding the whole after the disastrous breaking. Perhaps one day this will be the fate of Palestine too. It will become whole again, far more appreciated after going through wars and massacres before being reconstructed *kintsugi*-style.

It was not a bad start to the century. We celebrated New Year with a dancing party at our house. There were high hopes that Palestine would be making up for lost time and prospering. A most promising project then was the Bethlehem 2000 celebration, ably headed by a friend of mine, Nabeel Kassis, who had worked hard for two years to make this a success. Bethlehem 2000 aimed to launch Bethlehem and Palestine into the world through tourism promotion, capacity building and the preservation of cultural assets in the West Bank and Gaza. Nine months later our life irrevocably changed when, in September 2000, the Likud party leader, Ariel Sharon, marched up to the Haram al-Sharif, the site of the Dome of the Rock, the third holiest shrine in Islam, and sparked the second and more violent Intifada, shattering whatever peace we had managed to achieve. Since then we have not been able to reignite those hopes and everything seems to have gone inexorably downhill from there.

Leaving the house, I opened the outside gate, where a towering jacaranda hugged the wall, its feathery leaves studded with glorious bouquets of blue, bell-shaped flowers. I lingered to admire it before closing the gate, then descended the three steps from our house and started to walk to my office in the centre of town.

All the houses on our street, which is called Al Rabia (the hill), have low outside walls and gardens. Each is different. The house opposite is adorned with six Corinthian columns and has roses. The one right next door used to have a number of purple bougainvilleas falling over the wall, but since the death of the owner his widow has replaced them with a row of pencil cypresses that stand like sentinels, attempting to conceal the seating area at the front of the house but depriving the garden of that lush, expansive, exuberant look. Perhaps the widow decided bougainvillea was too messy; that garden is so neat and orderly, with umbrellas, garden tables and chairs. But the lawn has real grass, unlike most other gardens, which use an artificial grass-like covering imported from China. It's very different from ours, which in comparison looks like a jungle. Gardening style is a social indicator, though I refuse to be judged by it. A house further down the street used to have a thriving buddleia, which for some reason the owners decided to cut down and replace with a pittosporum that blooms in April and fills the street with a pleasant fragrance. In the front of the house there is a small unfilled pond and at the back a trampoline which is rarely, if ever, used.

As is the norm in Ramallah, all the houses are built from limestone. Those more recently constructed on the hill north of here are monumental in size. Not only do people show off with their sumptuous houses, but their front gardens with expensive palm trees are designed for the same purpose. The dilemma for those anxious to surround their houses with a high protective wall for security while hating to block the view of their garden is resolved by installing CCTV cameras. Ostentation is

not frowned upon here, despite the dire economic conditions that most people have to endure.

Across from where we live, the hills that remain visible between the houses reflect the sun in the late afternoon and glow pink. On humid mornings they fill up with mist.

As I make my way to the office I check the progress of the various gardens I pass. I feel weary. I was woken at three thirty by the Quranic readings, which were lengthy. They were followed by the call to prayer. And then, after I managed to return to sleep, another call to prayer. Everyone in the vicinity of the Al Taqwa (piety) mosque is in earshot of the speakers that boom out, yet no one is able to do anything about it. Frequently, when I'm writing, the *azan* (call to prayer) breaks my concentration. There is little doubt, to my mind, that the defeat of the nationalist project in Palestine by Israel that followed in the wake of the Oslo Accords encouraged the rise of political Islam, much like what happened elsewhere in the region. During the first Intifada in 1989, the UNRWA school not far from where we were living placed loudspeakers on its mosque. I called the principal, as did others, and objected to the noise. I said I expected a centre of learning to spread knowledge, not be a cause of annoyance to the neighbours. The principal eventually removed the loudspeakers.

Now we all – the entire neighbourhood – accept our fate in silence and are woken in the middle of the night by the zealous imam preceding the call to prayer with computer-recorded readings from the Quran. The two calls to prayer are made within a short interval, and the second ends with the statement that 'prayer is preferable to sleep'. I find it especially annoying that I should be instructed not to sleep. But what's the use: I'm already awake and must wait until the whole thing is over before I can try to get some more rest. When the tape finishes I hear the crackling static from the recording machine. All this is amplified with the help of ten loudspeakers decked around the exceptionally high minaret. And likewise the entire sermon and prayer from the mosque on Friday, when the sound is so loud I am unable to work. The sky is dominated by the prayer, as if we were living in some sort of seminary.

When I go shopping at the supermarket in the morning, rather than the lyrical voice of the much-loved Lebanese singer Fayrouz, I now hear Quranic readings. It took me a while to understand, but then I found that there is something hypnotic about these daytime readings. Hypnotic and relaxing. And so I've decided not to take this development as a personal defeat and have learned to live with it, adjusting my life accordingly and appreciating its meaning and effect on others as much as possible. Clearly religion has now become another weapon in the arsenal of struggle that is mobilised in the fight for self-assertion. The Palestinian villages next to Israeli settlements fill the air with the call to prayer to remind their unwanted neighbours that we're here and this is Palestinian land. In response, the Israeli reaction has been to attempt to pass a law prohibiting amplification of the call to prayer.

I see the traffic speeding by on Tireh Road and feel fortunate to have the time to walk to the office rather than drive. When I first moved here this road was not so busy. There were few houses beyond the top of the hill, north of where St George's School now sits. The pastoral has been turned into the urban and in the process the atmosphere of the place has been entirely transformed. Once a narrow, meandering road with many sharp turns, and fields of olive trees on both sides, led to the next tiny village of Ayn Qenia. The road used to be bordered by an ancient drystone wall that might have belonged to the nearby Byzantine *khirbeh* (ruins of an ancient settlement) called

Khirbet Al Tireh, which is now being excavated by archaeology students from Al Quds University. It's thought that the site is where St Stephen, venerated as the first Christian martyr, was once buried. You could walk along that narrow road and, just after the hill crested, Ramallah would come into view. It was a dramatic entrance to the sleepy city. One could linger to take in the scene without fear of being overrun by speeding cars, because there were fewer of them then. Now the wall has been demolished and the road widened from two to four lanes, so it is constantly busy with traffic leading to the numerous tall buildings that have arisen north of Ramallah, making the street ever busier with cars. In one such building, not far from here, the national poet Mahmoud Darwish lived until his death in 2013. His doctor had prescribed that he take a daily walk and I often encountered him near his house. I can still hear his deep melodious voice greeting me as our paths crossed.

Near where he lived was a small plant nursery, one of several that now exist in Ramallah. Many of the houses in my area have gardens, but only a few are worked on by their owners. Usually the gardens belong to rich mansions whose owners are too busy or too lazy to do the work and can afford to employ a gardener. You can always tell when this is the case. Such gardens do not reflect individual taste but follow the usual plan intended to make it look as eye-catching as possible from the outside. They have few of the indigenous plants like snapdragons, zinnias and geraniums; instead they boast fancy kinds that demand much water and care. Gardeners are in high demand, but they are not celebrities as in the UK. Gardening is still considered a lowly job. The owners of the two largest garden centres in the city, Abu Arab and Abu Zaki, have different attitudes to their work. Though knowledgeable about plants, Abu Arab, came from Jenin and is more interested in the commercial aspects of the business than in the plants. Not so Abu Zaki, a refugee living in

the Kalandia refugee camp. He worked for many years in Israel and knows only the Hebrew names for most of the plants he sells. Only in the last thirty years has Ramallah acquired garden centres. Before that, plants were shared and one got cuttings or planted from seed. Not so any more.

I come across a caper growing in the kerb, in the barely visible soil between the tarmac and the pavement, and I crouch to examine it. Its pods are just about to burst open. Walking, I am able to see and smell more. It makes me feel as though time has slowed down and I can linger on my way and examine things more closely. Gone are the anger and burning ambition that used to keep my mind so busy and distracted. It is as though I now have wings that make me feel lighter on my feet, able to float over the ground and look with unburdened eyes. No longer do I have to struggle for breath, as was the case in the past. Age might dull our senses but at least we're spared the doubt about who we are, our place and role in the world. This allows us to linger, take in the view and appreciate the beauty.

A year ago I was walking behind the Mustakbal School, northwest of here, and found a line of fossilised corals that formed what looked like a coral reef following the contour of the hills. Apparently it is possible to determine the depth of the water from the kind of animal fossils present. The tiny sea creatures from which corals were made lived near the surface, so where I found them must have once marked the level of the sea which aeons ago submerged these hills, which are composed of different kinds of limestone. I knew that the encroaching new buildings would destroy this line of fossils, so a few weeks ago I decided to go with my backpack and take as many of them as I could carry home with me. I also visited the place with my photographer friend Bassam Almohor, who photographed the fossils in situ. Soon enough, the bulldozer arrived and began to dig the land in preparation for new housing. I have no doubt that those who come to live here will have no inkling of what was there before they arrived. As I walk southward, downhill to my office, I will be descending deeper and deeper below what was once the waterline. Then, at the dip almost halfway down Tireh Road, I will begin to climb another of Ramallah's many hills.

In December 2001 the Israeli army made its first limited incursion into Ramallah since the signing of the Oslo Accords. A tank was parked at the corner of our street and Tireh Road, close to the empty house of Ziadeh Shamieh, who has lived for most of his adult life in the US. I remember bringing my seven-year-old nephew Aziz to look at the tank, so that when the Israeli invasion of Ramallah, which seemed imminent, started he would not be too shocked and realise that there were human beings inside these monsters. As we walked back towards my house, I asked Aziz whether he would like to look inside the little room: 'Shall we ask permission from the soldier to go in?' He looked at me with his large, intelligent eyes as though I was utterly mad. 'No,' he said, with a knowing grin to indicate that he realised I could not be serious, and tried to get me to walk away faster.

For many years since then I have tried to influence his thinking, but now I know that he, at twenty-two, will make his own choices and find his own way of relating to the political struggle. It is folly to believe that, just as when you get higher up a hill you can see more, adding years will bring clarity. And if that is true, why should he be interested in my clarity or my truth? Surely the future is his; my past is of no consequence to him, nor can I assume that it is an inspiration. There is little about it that's heroic. It's more a chronicle of repeated failures. Both we and the Israelis who were against the settlement project have failed to find a way of living together and that's the biggest tragedy. Now time is running out.

Growing in the garden of the house on a side road there is a blooming jacaranda whose petals shining in the morning sun attracts my attention and distracts me from my angry thoughts about the tank. I turn and walk down to have a closer look. It stands in the garden of a four-storey building where a micro-finance office with the nice acronym FATEN operated. It's one of many lending agencies and banks giving small loans, a product of the last twenty years, during which most Palestinians have become debtors. Prior to 1995, when the Oslo Accord was signed, there were no banks offering mortgages and ownership of a single flat in a communally owned building was not possible. Since then we have had a large number of banks that dispense loans freely. It is said that 80 per cent of society are in debt. This might help explain why no commercial strike has been called, even on a day like this. I stood under the tree, admiring its floral bouquets. It was entirely full of blossoms, with no leaves. There are two kinds of jacaranda, one where the leaves and blossom come out at the same time and another where the blossoms come first, filling the tree with their splendour, and only later do the leaves follow. Ours was the former sort. Fortunately for this tree, it blossoms in June, when there are few competitors, so it gets all the attention. These trees are recent arrivals; there were none in Ramallah prior to the occupation.

I climbed back up to Al Rabia Street and walked a short distance. Just before I turned the corner where the French bakery opened a few years ago, on my right was St George's School, a single-block drab building like a prison with high walls topped by wire mesh. It was built by the Greek Orthodox church on a small plot of land. The church is dominated by the Greek patriarchs. Over the years, many Palestinians bequeathed their land to the church, which became rich, owning large tracts. But rather than build the school on a more spacious plot, the church acted in a miserly fashion, behaving as though they were giving the Palestinians charity. Centuries-long efforts by the local congregation to win control of the church have never succeeded. And the Greeks, who are in the higher clerical ranks, have remained unaccountable, acting as sole owners, misusing church property and often selling assets while keeping the church archives under lock and key, never allowing any researcher access in order to reveal the secret deals made over the years. The school day had already begun and I could hear through the wide-open windows the teacher instructing his pupils in a loud commanding voice to repeat after him the lesson of the day.

The first school I ever visited as a child, the Friends Girls' School, had a much more attractive campus full of trees. It was next to our house in the old city of Ramallah, where I grew up. I had gone there with Adeeba, my mother's domestic helper. I remember well that first visit. It was a cold December late morning. I was rarely let out of the house on cold days in winter, so this was exceptional. I took Adeeba's hand and together we walked in the fog. There was no one else on the street in this old part of town. I held tightly to her hand as she proceeded with stately steps in silence. She was always silent. She had a white *mandeel* (scarf) that covered her hair and went down to her shoulders which she fixed on her head with a pin. I was going to school to eat lunch with my sisters. They woke up early every morning and prepared for school. I woke with them, but refused to eat my egg. It was disgusting. I could not eat. I didn't want to eat. My mother said I must if I was to grow up to be a man. My mother prepared food for my sisters and put it in the tiffin-tin lunch boxes for Adeeba to take to them. That day she made the decision to send me along, hoping that in the company of other kids I would agree to eat. She had tried all her usual tricks – playing games, telling me stories to distract me as she fed me one spoon at a time – but nothing worked.

Everything was transformed by the fog. Our neighbour Nur's fig tree seemed to be breathing clouds out of its branches. On the other side of the street, Jaber's pistachio shrubs looked more dense. The tops of the pine trees in our garden were invisible. We walked through the small door into the school campus. The wind howled and made the branches of the enormous pine trees sway from side to side. I was wearing several jumpers and a coat, a scarf and a woollen hat, which were dampened by the fog. The school grounds were deserted. We went straight to the kindergarten building with its big arching windows painted yellow, where there was the happy buzz of small children running around. It had different-coloured low tables and small chairs. We found my sisters sitting at one of the tables. I was glad to see them. Their teachers were milling around. We found two more chairs and Adeeba put the lunch boxes on the table. My sisters looked embarrassed by these visitors from home. Tall Adeeba seemed out of place, her large body perched on a small chair. I sat close to her among the other children. She made me feel safe. I was happy to be here. The windows were misty and the room was warm. We began to eat. I was glad to eat now. I was still eating when an old woman with a tight bun on her head came over to us. She stooped and put her downy face close to mine. But I didn't want an old person near me. I was now with my sisters and the young children around them, happy together. Why did she have to come and scare us?

I waited to see whether my sisters would do anything about this menace, but they didn't. They sat quietly, politely tolerating her, so she went on disturbing our happy little world. I felt I had to do something about this. So I stood up, went around this monster and, reaching as high as I could, kicked it from behind as hard as I could, to make her go away. I didn't want her there. She straightened her back and left us, laughing. I looked to see whether my sisters were relieved because I had saved them. But

I could tell they were embarrassed. Why? Had I not done the right thing?

Before I left, Ahmad, the school carpenter, showed me the little house he had made. He was dark and had uneven yellow teeth and small, gloomy black eyes. The doll's house was on a pedestal and had tiny windows and furniture inside. Fascinated, I took a peek through the windows. Ahmad's serious face was next to mine and I could see his gold front tooth.

I wanted to go to school like my sisters and be in this big room, sitting on these small colourful chairs. But I didn't want to have the old woman come around to scare me. I only wanted to be happy with other children.

On our way back we had to cross the street to avoid meeting the old man we called *shawish* (lieutenant), with his heavy green army coat that looked like something worn by Ottoman soldiers during the First World War. He lived in a broken-down Volkswagen Beetle, like a hedgehog. He never spoke, though there were rumours about his violent outbursts, which were like being attacked by quills. We also never knew where he came from (though rumours abounded that he had fought in the Second World War). Then one day he was no longer there and his home was removed from the pavement.

We passed St Joseph School and could see the nuns inside through the wire fence. Their garden had a row of strikingly white arum lilies with their egg-yolk-yellow stamens which we called Mar Yousef flowers. Along the wire fence was blue morning glory. We also passed the tile makers and the blacksmith and, closer to our house, Nur's field, where she planted tomatoes in the summer. Nur had small brown eyes and her skin was wrinkled like the ripe figs that grew on her tree.

The first question my mother asked when we got home was whether I had finished my plate. Adeeba announced that I had. As always, I was glad to make my mother happy.

After he immigrated to the US and established a successful restaurant in Houston, a former classmate of mine, Albert Rukab, whose family owns the famous ice-cream parlour in Ramallah, told me that he found it strange how he, who as a child gave his mother such a hard time refusing to eat, ended up preparing all these meals for others. 'How often do I stand in the busy kitchen and think to myself: what would my mother say if she saw me now?' I too have passed through a huge transformation and have since acquired a passion for food and enjoy cooking. I sometimes think that my obsession with eating well is my way of warding off the ravaging years.

Three

I turned the corner and walked uphill along Tireh Road. Up the street was a petrol station owned by a man with many sons, judging by the large number of commercial ventures that keep popping up there: a drive-in café, a hardware shop, a grocery. I can imagine that the head of this large family feels he has to find employment for his children. Where there is no government to take care of its citizens, the father has to provide.

When I made the appointment at my office I was aware that it was the fiftieth anniversary of the occupation. Past anniversaries have been commemorated with demonstrations and a commercial strike. Today I wasn't expecting much to happen, though it was possible that protests had been planned that I wasn't aware of. That's why I had decided to go early, to have time to cancel the appointment if it proved difficult for my client to reach the office.

In other years I had passed this anniversary hiking in the nearby hills. After a short walk I would leave the town behind me. That's no longer possible. The hills have been invaded. My only alternative is an urban walk. I have a few hours before my one-thirty meeting. I will take the longer route to my office, which is normally only a forty-five-minute walk from my house; this will make it four hours.

As I walk, once again I can hear readings from the Quran from the nearby mosque. When the Quran is recited in a melodious voice it is enchanting. Now that it's already eight days since the start of this year's holy month of Ramadan, the readings seem to go on almost continuously throughout the day. It is no longer possible to enjoy those quiet mornings that Ramallah was famous for. If it's not the call to prayer, then it's the screeching of speeding cars on Tireh Road or the buzz of Israeli surveillance planes up in the sky. The verses being recited proclaim that God, the all-knowing, who neither begets nor is begotten, knows all about you and bids you to pray and will punish you for your neglect, but then God is also forgiving. It was He who created the earth and sky in six days. Out there is a community with a holistic view of society, of the beginning and the end, to which it must feel good to belong. What would it be like to have that unquestioning sense of belonging and a strong religious belief?

Last night we had dinner at the Snowbar garden restaurant with a Palestinian friend who holds a Jerusalem identity card and has applied for one for her husband, otherwise they cannot continue to live together in Jerusalem. The application, known as family reunion, was submitted a long time ago. Penny asked her about the progress of her application. 'I found out that the head of the Israeli Interior Ministry office is a woman who grew up in East Jerusalem in a house confiscated from a Palestinian family,' she responded. Penny winked at me but neither of us said anything and I did not mention that I knew her father when he worked in Ramallah at the military government. I remembered how, when I first met him, he was so hard up he wore different-coloured socks.

How extensive has been Israel's success. This woman who now lives in a Jewish settlement in the West Bank is working in the department that exercises so much power over us and determines which Palestinian can or cannot live in the city of their birth with their spouse. Not only have we failed to end the occupation, but every year it seems to be ever more entrenched. Almost daily now we hear of killings of young men who attempt to stab Israelis. On the one hand there's chaos and mayhem and on the other, the certainty and order that religious teachings offer. Is it any wonder that more are flocking in the direction of religion?

For many years I was too involved in politics to notice my surroundings. I felt my very survival was at stake and this was distracting enough. Now that I realise the limits of my abilities to make any effective change in the way the struggle is conducted, I no longer feel like this and have more leisure to think of myself in the world, of my body in time. Many men my age talk only about their physical afflictions. I avoid doing that and yet I'm all too aware of the passing of time.

I could feel a few drops of rain on my head. How strange that it should rain in June. No sooner had the rain fallen than the air was saturated with that peculiar odour that comes wafting up from the ground just after the rain. June is unquestionably the best month in Ramallah, when the weather is moderate and the greenery in the hills has not yet been burned dry. I can enjoy the morning to the fullest. The jacarandas are in bloom and the sky is bedecked with clouds that partially conceal the late spring sun. Soon, without our taking notice, spring will segue into summer.

A few weeks ago Penny and I visited a photography exhibition at the Israel Museum in Jerusalem called *1967*. The first photograph showed a frontal view of one of Israel's military leaders, the then defence minister, Moshe Dayan, instantly recognisable by the eyepatch over his left eye. It was taken during a visit he made at the beginning of the occupation to the Kalandia refugee camp near Jerusalem. In it Dayan has a self-assured, piercing gaze like that of a hawk. To a large extent, Israeli history has been determined by daring leaders like Dayan. We wouldn't be in our sad predicament if it were not for the decision by such leaders to pre-empt the war in June 1967 with Egypt and Syria by striking first and destroying their air force before they could make a single sortie. The war which was supposed to have lasted for six days but was in fact won by Israel in less time resulted in the Israeli occupation of Sinai, the Golan Heights, the West Bank (including eastern Jerusalem) and the Gaza Strip.

What if this tactic had not worked? What if Israel had not achieved such a total victory, humiliating the neighbouring Arab countries and emerging so impregnable, a superstar. And to our misfortune, all this happened when the US, Israel's ally, was losing in its war in Vietnam. No wonder that Israel became the darling idol of the Americans and won even more support than it had earlier enjoyed. Decades of air supremacy followed, allowing Israel to behave not only as the strongest power in the skies of the Middle East, but as the only one.

Following the generals who proudly surveyed the territory they had conquered came the sweaty, bearded, fat men wearing dark coats who looked at our hills with a covetous eye and decided that this was where their prophets had walked, where they would establish their settlements, taking the land free of charge and using money from the US to build them. They haven't stopped doing that for the past half-century.

This morning I had read that there are negotiations with Israel to allow buses to leave Ramallah through the Beitunia checkpoint, now called Ofer, to take worshipers to pray at Al Aqsa mosque in Jerusalem during Ramadan. My first reaction was happiness. Then I realised I've become so used to the closure of the outlet from Beitunia to Palestinian traffic, begun a decade ago, and have so internalised the new geography Israel has succeeded in imposing, that this sounded extraordi- ✓ nary to me. How readily we accept the outrageous terms of our confinement: residents of East Jerusalem may not live in the West Bank and those of the West Bank and Gaza Strip may not change their place of residence even if they get married to a spouse from another area in Palestine.

I used to drive to Jerusalem through Beitunia all the time before this prohibition. It was there on that narrow quiet road that I learned to drive, before Israel constructed the six-lane settler road that connects the northwestern Jewish settlements to the coastal region, bisecting the road on which I used to drive. After I got my licence I would borrow my sister's Opel Kadett in the afternoon and stop to look at what I called the yellow house. It lay in a sea of dry yellow wheat that surrounded it on all sides, except for the small garden with a meandering path and two tall sunflower plants that stood by the gate like sentinels. In the late afternoon the rays of the low sun on the horizon would be reflected on the dull yellow limestone, making the whole house glow like the moon.

At this time of year, the end of spring, the pond formed by the runoff water in the low plain would have shrunk and all around it farmers would have planted cucumbers of the ordinary and Armenian kinds and tomato seedlings. Soon we would be driving there to buy those utterly delicious and healthy *ba'li* (unirrigated) organic vegetables. How changed and inaccessible the area has become. Where the yellow house stood there is now an ever-expanding Israeli settlement called Givat Ze'ev, where we cannot set foot. The cultivated plain has vanished and been replaced by an army barracks and the Ofer military court and prison.

Earlier, when I walked past St George's School, I noticed that the students have yet again scrawled on the wall, 'Nadeem Nowara we shall never forget you.' Three years ago their fellow student went to demonstrate against the practice of administrative detention close to Ofer prison and was callously shot dead. A CNN video shows the moment the unarmed youth was shot by an Israeli soldier, Ben Deri, who later said he did it because he was bored. Using live ammunition and pointing straight at Nadeem Nowara, Deri clearly intended to kill. The young man can be seen walking with his arms at his sides, then a soldier standing on the wall shot him. The bullet struck the seventeen-year-old in the chest, causing him to do a somersault, first falling forward on his hands and then, as his hands buckled, falling backward like an antelope shot mid-leap. Near where the first Christian martyr once lay is one of Palestine's youngest.

The army denied using live ammunition. It was only because Nadeem's father hid the bullet that had lodged in his son's backpack that it was impossible for the army to refute what happened. After four years of legal wrangling, Deri was sentenced to nine months' imprisonment, which the Supreme Court in Israel doubled to eighteen. Meanwhile Nadeem's class-mates had to contend with an empty desk where their friend used to sit.

This seventeen-year-old was too young to have known what the area was like before the settlement was constructed: what habitat it provided for the migrating birds that stopped in Ramallah on their way north to drink and bathe, and what a great attraction for all of us it was to see a body of water in the midst of our arid land. He was too young to have tasted the *ba'li* organic vegetables that used to be grown there. When I look at the Ofer checkpoint I see both how it is now and what it was like before the area was ruined. For me it was an open road, for them a border. For me and my generation the struggle has aged, become blocked, just like that road is blocked. I know how it used to be, but I don't know how to unblock it and allow the life that was once there to thrive again. For Nadeem and his generation they never had that memory. They only know it as it has now become. In the intensification of the violence, they have lost one of their classmates, an experience that I never had. They glorify him as a *shaheed* (martyr) to lessen the blow, yet the fact remains, which they cannot ignore, that he is no more. Had we succeeded in resolving this conflict we would have saved ourselves and the world from its ugly consequences.

Rather than stand at the edge of the pond and watch the migrating birds, their *shaheed* could see only walls and barbed wire surrounding a military prison where administrative detainees, many as young as him, are locked up, on whose behalf he had gone to demonstrate. Some of the detainees have been there for over a year and none have been on the new road that links the settlement to the northeast of Jerusalem with the coast, where yet another new border has been set up.

The landscape familiar to me as I was growing up is no more; it has changed, as has the cast of characters, both Israeli and Palestinian. The legal strategies we employed to resist the occupation, believing they would bring it to an end, have dismally failed. The changes brought about over the past half-century have created a new overwhelming reality that calls for a different approach and a new kind of leadership. For us who have aged with the struggle, it's time we recognise our defeat, step aside, hand over the reins to the young and place our hope in them.

I was nearly Nadeem's age in 1967, when the war that brought about this half-century-long occupation took place. Few Palestinians in the West Bank took part in the fighting. For nineteen years the regime in Jordan made sure that we did not have a single weapon, or any military training to speak of. So what kind of victory was Israel's? Why be so arrogant about it?

It was as though we had been slumbering, had abandoned our fate to others and were looking at ourselves from a distance. Then we were rudely awakened by a strange, short war that did not feel like a war, at least not where I was. It started and ended in the blink of an eye and our unwanted, unrecognised neighbours from across the horizon came and took over our lives.

Even after the passage of fifty years I can still recall so clearly that fateful day when the Israeli army entered my city. It was announced by incessant shooting that began just after sunset, a sort of loud and assertive proclamation of the changing of the guard. From the sound of their bullets I attempted to figure out how close the soldiers were to our house. They must already be at the top of the slope. I imagined them approaching our garden gate. How many of them were there? It was not possible to tell. There was a brief pause in the shooting. Were they trying to enter? As the shooting got closer, I could feel my father becoming more anxious. My mother was quiet but obviously fretful. I remained silent and still, trying my best not to show how scared I was. Between the bursts of gunfire I could hear my parents' heavy breathing. Was this the end? Would the soldiers shoot their way into our house and massacre us all, or was this only going to be the fate of the men, my father and me? My brother was still too young to be considered a man.

Though the soldiers seemed not to be moving, the shooting intensified. What point could they be making? Why were they lingering at the gate? What did they suspect? Our garden must be covered with empty shells by now. Time seemed to stop. How quickly a safe and friendly place can become vulnerable and hostile. It had never occurred to me that the windows in our house could be conduits for danger. Even the stone walls felt flimsy.

When we woke up next morning everything was surprisingly calm. Nothing in our house was broken, not a single window. The weather was crisp and clear. It was one of those lovely early June days, like today, that Ramallah is known for. At first it seemed like any other June morning – the birds were chirruping, the sun was out – except it wasn't. We had just been through a war, one that we had lost, and our town was taken over by the enemy.

The army drove around with bullhorns ordering us, residents of the town, to raise a white flag. I can still see *Tata's* (grandmother's) large white underwear billowing on the clothes line on her kitchen balcony.

After they drove away there was a strange quality to the atmosphere that descended. Members of the Jordanian army, with their thick moustaches and heavy boots, had disappeared, their absence leaving a profound silence. They were replaced by last night's shooters, who now drove around victoriously in their dusty jeeps, announcing curfews. Only when I looked at the ground could I confirm that it was all real, for the garden was carpeted with empty bullet shells, yellow against the brown soil. I had not dreamed the events of the night before.

It was several days before the round-the-clock curfew was lifted, but only for a few hours in the morning to allow us to shop. This was the first time we were able to venture into the centre of town and examine the damage. There wasn't much. Here and there a few shop windows were broken, with glass scattered over the pavements. Some electricity and telephone poles lay on the ground, with the cables spread dangerously around. This seemed to be all. But it was enough to indicate that the town had been disgraced. It looked stunted and stopped. Not only cables down but also the residents' spirits. Pedestrians no longer walked with pride. They scurried with their heads bent down, scrutinising the ground before them, anxious to finish what business they had to do in the short time they were allowed out of the house. The magic that had permeated the town before the war was gone. Defeat was painted all over the place. The sense that our town was no longer ours was hard to take.

It was as though the city had been defiled, taken over by foreigners who did not appreciate its charm, worth and uniqueness. In run-down cars the euphoric Israeli civilians drove around, checking how our side looked, describing it as just another ramshackle backwater. The pride I had in my city quickly vanished. It now felt abandoned – even though most of its residents had stayed, they seemed to have disappeared indoors. If a city can look bewildered, this is how I imagined Ramallah to be. Only men walked hurriedly in the street when curfew was lifted. A friend once told me that village men feel embarrassed to walk in the street next to a woman, so you would always see their wives trailing behind. Now the women were nowhere to be seen. They stayed home as the men went out for some relief from their enforced detention in their houses and to check how many had died and assess the damage that had been done to their town. The men looked lost as they walked in the windswept streets. The Grand Hotel, which had been the showpiece of the town, where guests from all over the region flocked to visit, was now the headquarters of the Israeli military in Ramallah. Soldiers slept in the rooms that had welcomed tourists and honeymooning couples. We were not allowed anywhere near the grounds. The post office was also commandeered and all government offices. The cinemas were closed, as was Uncle Sam's café, where young couples went for hot chocolate. Its coloured-glass windows, through which it was just possible to make out their outlines, huddled over the narrow tables eating pastries and drinking, were now broken. The whole town looked desolate. All those places that I had enjoyed, or was waiting to frequent when I came of age, were now closed. Little was left of the Ramallah I had known. The only people smiling on the streets were the Israeli soldiers.

The question that seemed to worry my father was who would clean up the debris and repair what was broken now that the municipality was unable to take charge. In every sense the town seemed abandoned to those who had conquered it. It was no longer ours.

The town's elected mayor, Nadeem Zarou, was deported. The soldiers allowed him to stop at our house on his way to the Allenby Bridge, the crossing point to Jordan, to bid my father farewell. Mockingly he told my father, 'I will be sending you my photograph.' Although we were not told that he was being deported, we took this to mean that he did not expect ever to return, though he did, after the Oslo Accords were signed. In his place the military appointed a new mayor, a weak yes-man who would do as he was told.

They came from the west, proud and arrogant Israelis: flushed with victory, bragging about how developed, orderly and democratic their country was. It was as though we had exchanged borders. We now became open to the west and closed to the east, exposed and unprotected. In the aftermath of victory, the streets in Israel were full of people basking in the glory of their triumph. Their appetite for the land in the West Bank became insatiable. And yet despite the fact that we were defeated in the war, there was not the usual infatuation with the coloniser, no desire to learn their language or become like them. Nor did Israel encourage this. All they wanted was that we leave.

Many of those who tried to lord it over me, whether it was the military governors of my town, Avi or Roni, or the legal advisers, Axel or Yossi, are either dead or elderly now. They were gone before I had the opportunity to enquire whether they had any regrets about the policies they were enforcing, which are now bringing ruin to their country. Perhaps the confidence of those Israeli colonisers lasted a lifetime. It is folly to think they could have felt any remorse. Those of them who are no more would have died, like all of us will die, thinking primarily of themselves, the world reduced to their failing body, neither proud of their achievements nor harbouring contrition for crimes committed and suffering caused. 'This is the way the world ends, not with a bang but a whimper.' Weak and frail is the son of man. It is just my unbridled optimism that makes me think it could be otherwise, just another version of believing there is a heavenly place where justice prevails.

And yet a time will surely come when a revisionist history of the conflict will be written revealing how they failed, how their perceived victories, freeing the military and the Jewish settler movement from the shackles of Israeli and international law to facilitate the building of more Jewish settlements, led to disaster. But they will be long gone. To them it will not matter.

At sixteen I was on the receiving end of the euphoria of an enemy who just a short while before had feared for its very existence. I could not have imagined then that I would spend the next half-century of my life under their sway. For many years I raged in anger at my fate. Now, when I look back over my life, I can see that the occupation has provided me with an immense amount of work and great challenges, not only in how to resist but in how to live under its ruthless matrix of control as a free man refusing to be denied the joys of life.

Four

When I was growing up, Ramallah had few restaurants and a number of men-only coffee shops where mainly old men wearing ancient dark suits sat around on low wicker stools and played backgammon, drank coffee and smoked. These days the city is celebrated for its hundreds of cafés and restaurants, and Tireh Road, where I was now walking, had no fewer than nine, plus an ice-cream parlour called Sticks, offering 'home-made Italian gelato'. Unlike Rukab's, the solitary ice-cream place in Ramallah in my youth, which opened only in the spring and summer months because it was thought no one would want ice cream in winter, Sticks remains open all year round. Male and female staff serve in these cafés. The first that I came across, just after passing the Office of the People's Republic of China, was Al Reef, which was established in that strange garden of Abu Ameen's, in whose house we lived before we built our present home. Just beyond the restaurant is a still-undeveloped plot with olive trees. I remembered that during the Intifada Israeli soldiers cut down the trees to protect settlers who were using this road to get from Dolev to Beit El. A yellow line was painted on the road to lead them along. The line has now gone and the resilient trees have grown back. They seem to produce a better crop than the olive trees in my garden, because the dust and soot from the car exhausts cover the blossoms and protect them from birds and disease. But there's no doubt that they will soon be destroyed forever and a new building will go up in their place. Then this street will become even busier.

Further up on the left-hand side of the street is an old abandoned house, a likely candidate for demolition. The land around it was being exploited by an enterprising man and his son, who either own it or have reached an agreement with the owner to use it as a herb garden. They have ploughed and fertil-ised the plot and divided it into beds, where they plant parsley and rocket, which they then sell from a stall on the nearby pavement. I've often admired the healthy greens growing there and wondered how they are able to keep them free of weeds. Perhaps the farmer had a way of dealing with the weed problem that I could use in my garden. One afternoon I decided to stop and ask. The man did not take kindly to my question and thought I was either an utter fool or pulling his leg. In a voice indicating what a ludicrous question I'd asked, he said with a straight face, 'Sit on your bum and pull out the weeds, one by one.'

Two-thirds of the way up this road was the den of the Ramallah scouts, called the First Ramallah Group. It was given this name because it couldn't get recognition as a scout group since Palestine was not a state. It now has an Olympic-sized swimming pool and a garden café. In 1971 I participated in the first international work camp in Ramallah that landscaped the garden. The tents where we slept were put up in the area where the pool was later built, organised by Issa Mughanam, a much-loved teacher who always kept his deformed left hand in his pocket, out of sight. Now there are a number of public swimming pools all over the city in the numerous gyms and garden restaurants, some of them even heated in winter. Close by is a house that seems abandoned with a large front garden. It used to be the last house in this northern part of the city. In the garden a patch of irises continues to grow and produce the most beautiful light blue, rabbit-ear irises each April. I've frequently been tempted to go in and dig out some of the bulbs.

There was a time when I used to know to whom every house belonged. Across the street from the scout centre, at the corner of Tireh and Jabra Ibrahim Jabra roads, the latter named after the Palestinian writer, is the house where the poet Lily Karniek lived until her death. She led an outwardly uneventful life with her mother, teaching Arabic at an UNRWA school. Her father used to collect the offerings at our church.

Down this road is a semi-detached, single-storey stone house where I lived from 1979 to 1988, after returning from my law studies in London. A few days ago I dreamed of that house. The dream has stayed with me because, unlike the recurring dream when I go in search of a house, this was a return to where I had actually lived in my twenties and early thirties. In this dream I saw Helen, the landlady, sitting with her friend, the mathematics teacher Georgette, chatting and smoking, as was their wont, with the front door wide open. When they saw me coming they began clearing the house to give it back to me. I thought perhaps I would stay. As I stepped inside, a slim leopard leapt out through the open kitchen door as soon as he saw me enter. I walked around the empty house, then decided it was too cold and had no furniture, and so I left to go and sleep at my parents' house. When I woke I wondered whether the alert animal that I saw darting out represented my younger self.

In the late 1970s, moving out of the family house before getting married was not common in conservative Ramallah. Hence there was no community of young people living on their own. Society was very family-orientated. The path to adulthood that society charted was unflinchingly clear: first, work to raise enough money to get settled, then marriage and children and, if possible, construct your own house. But at that point in my life I did not want any of this. Instead I wanted to emulate what I believed had been my father's way of life as a young bachelor, which I imagined to be the ideal life. Though doing so did not make me feel closer to my father, I did, however, buck the trend and choose to live alone, in this stone dwelling, determined to pay no heed to prevailing social norms.

I was relieved to find my house still standing, though it was now abandoned. Helen had died several years ago, and was already a widow when I rented from her. Her husband had been a political activist with the Communist Party and had spent many years in prison. 'He gave me a lot of heartache,' she once confided. After her death, her two sons emigrated to the US. At some point they will, no doubt, look to sell the house, which will fetch a high price because of the scarcity of land. Whoever buys the property will surely demolish it and use the expensive land to construct a building as high as the law allows.

Helen was an efficient, kind and progressive working woman who never interfered with me or objected to the loud music I often played or the gatherings of friends that sometimes lasted late into the night, even though the flat that I rented shared a wall with hers. Nor to my knowledge did she comment on or gossip about my strange behaviour. In this two-room flat I tried to create a home for myself, decorating it in the manner that pleased me. I went through a phase when I smoked pot. I would close the flimsy curtains and then, concealed from the outside, escape into my own world. Sitting cross-legged in a yoga position, I would slip into various parts of my body, experiencing new sensations and passions whirling in me as I sought to still the turbulence and find my equilibrium. But they

were only flimsy curtains offering limited respite until the next
incursion and interruption.

So determined was I to protect my privacy that when my
father insisted that I get a phone I banished it to the laundry
basket and never admitted to having one. Then one day while a
friend was visiting it rang. I had forgotten to disconnect it and
so out of the laundry basket came the sound of ringing. I sat
still, showing no sign of awareness of the offensive intrusion,
seemingly oblivious to the persistent sound. 'Aren't you going
to answer it?' my friend asked. In a desperate effort to keep my
secret, I claimed that it was the neighbour's phone. She was too
bright to be taken in by this, but too polite to contradict me as
we both sat waiting for the ringing to stop.

The windows of the abandoned house were now concealed
by the overgrown shrubs entangled in the iron bars. How like a
cocoon, I thought, as I looked at it from the outside.

One afternoon in 1980 I remember returning home and
realising that I did not have my front door key. I had lent my car
to my brother, Samer, and forgotten to take the house key from
the key-chain I handed over to him. As I waited for him to bring
back the car, I stood there before the closed curtains, observing
the house from the outside. Now, with the windows concealed
by shrubs, it was all coming back.

The more I looked, the more I felt that the house resembled
me. The simplicity of the place was deliberate. I had come back
intending to live an alternative, non-material lifestyle. I made
a simple bed from blocks of wood on which I mounted a thin
sheet of plywood (which I could remove and lean against the
wall when the bedroom was transformed into a dance floor).
I also made a bookshelf which kept tumbling down. I did not
want to be a lawyer who shared the material values of other
lawyers. I wanted to avoid ostentatious living, to better relate
to my society, seeking to be closer to them through living

like an ordinary person, simply. It was here in this house that, as a young man, I lived a life of rebellion against all sorts of conventions and materialism. I was unappreciative of father's expressed wish to have grandchildren. I didn't feel he had the right to expect this of me when I was not ready. I wanted to be free to live with little and walk in the hills, which at the time was not something that others did. My father thought I was self-indulgent and told me so. 'You simply don't want to be bothered,' he said. At the same time I wanted to practise law – wear the tailored suits I had brought from London and go to court, donning the barrister's black robe that I had also carried back with me. On such occasions I would wear my serious, authoritative face and proceed to play the part of the lawyer. This did not mean that I neglected my other two roles as the human rights activist who exposed Israeli violations and the writer who wrote about ordinary Palestinians carrying on with their daily lives under Israeli occupation. I had no time to waste. I proceeded with all the energy I could muster to do the work, paying no heed to what society around me thought. This was precisely what worried my father.

During the day I wanted to be serious and work hard. At the weekend I wanted to enjoy my other interests, preserving my frivolous side and expressing that playful, juvenile aspect of my character that was still refusing to grow up. If only my father could have understood that it was the time in my life, late in arriving, when I wanted to regain and live the lost opportunities that usually come at an earlier age but which, with the onset of the occupation and the periods of prolonged curfews when I was sixteen, had to be postponed.

I was also working on my writing, which required distance. But solitude was deemed disrespectful, weird or ill-mannered and could only indicate that I was elitist, angry or deranged. Who would choose to live alone? people wondered – unless there was something genuinely wrong with him or he was on bad terms with his family.

There was a small garden at the back of the house which got little sun and had terrible soil, yet, ever the enthusiastic gardener, I tried to make the most of it. But it didn't really matter if little grew there because the hills all around the house were a natural wild garden that was lovely in all seasons, with different colours throughout the year. Right next to the door there was a shrub with graceful yellow flowers which in Arabic are called *asafeer al janneh* (birds of paradise). Out of a slab of rock a fig tree grew. In the midst of so much chaos and confusion, fear and uncertainty, I managed to ensure isolated moments of calm, peace and beauty.

At this period I spent a lot of time researching the legal violations the Israeli occupation was committing. I became a vocal advocate for human rights. As I looked at my former house by the fig tree, its windows now almost covered by the branches of the shrubs and trees growing in the garden, in my mind's eye I could still see the floor carpeted with copies of military orders spread over the tiles in preparation for my testimony before the Geneva-based UN Committee investigating Israeli practices in the occupied territories. During that time in my life I had felt like a man obsessed, privy to information which had escaped others and which it was incumbent upon me to make known, and make known now, before the practices of the occupation, such as the Jewish settlements, became entrenched and it would be too late.

Back then I believed that people wore their serious faces, as I did, at will, like a mask they could just as easily drop. I remember, when I was a student in the ninth grade, stepping into the office of the dean, Mr Farid Tabri, and being unable to stop giggling at his serious face. There he was in his office, all alone and with little to do, so he did not need to put on such a pinched, scary look. I had assumed that his serious face, with the two parallel lines engraved on his cheeks, was to keep us at bay, to intimidate us and put us in our place. Surely, when he retired alone to his office, he relaxed and perhaps managed a smile? To see him with that face when there was no one around to frighten seemed so incongruous that I could not stop giggling.

I wanted to be multi-faced, with one face for when I was with my friends, another for the courts of law and another for when I was advocating for human rights. For the longest time when I lived in that house, I was trying on those different masks.

I would walk in the hills to relieve that grip over my features, starting with the face. As I walked or sat under an olive tree, I would feel each part of my face in turn relaxing, the unclenching of my teeth, the easing of the pressure in my eyes, the slow release of the sides of my mouth that had been held tight to retain the serious expression. Then the rest of the muscles in my body would, one by one, begin to loosen up. I could feel my stomach muscles soften and my shoulders expand after being hunched from hours at my typewriter. Returned to myself, I would begin to look and feel like a different man.

In the silence of Helen's house I also worked on writing a humorous book in which I made fun of everything, of myself and my work, which I was fond of describing as that of an administrative guerrilla. Alone, I would laugh at everything, but primarily at myself and how seriously I was taking matters. Now, after fifty years of occupation, settlements are no longer a mere possibility but a defining reality. And so it makes no sense to laugh them off. Our horizons have narrowed as the prospects for peace have vanished. I've aged, as has the present cast of characters at the top of the Palestinian political ladder. Our only hope is in the next generation.

Yet even when I thought I was a rebel I still had an inflated sense of myself, believing that my work posed a threat to the

Israeli authorities. I presumed that I was under surveillance and that it was likely that Israel would try and do away with my life, or that of my friends, as they had done to many prominent and effective Palestinians who participated in the struggle.

Once, just before midnight, I was saying goodbye to a friend, Ellen Cantarow, when we heard ticking near the fuel tank of her rented car. We became worried that the car would explode when she started it. We kept circling that vehicle, trying to figure out the cause of that ticking. I finally decided to take my chance, despite the lateness of the hour, and knocked on the door of a neighbour who owned a garage. He was kind enough to check and calm us down. But then when he invited us in we got stuck with him as he raged against the occupation, directing the full brunt of his anger at my American friend. We sat there and listened to his explosive diatribe directed mainly against her country. He spoke so fast that he barely paused for breath. We felt like hostages. It was well past midnight when we were finally able to extricate ourselves from his clutches and Ellen started her car without any further explosions from either this angry man or that imaginary ticking bomb.

My former home is now dwarfed by the tall buildings all around it. The road leading to it used to stop a few metres from my house but now continues all the way down to Wadi Al Kalb, with buildings on either side. Long gone is that old meandering track following the contours of the hills which I used to follow down to the wadi. The last time I visited the wadi I noticed that all the springs had dried up. Much of the rainwater that used to seep through the bare earth to feed these springs can no longer do so due to the massive amount of building and the paving of the roads that have sealed the earth above. Also gone are those wonderful days when I could just take off and walk in the hills, down to the valley along the old paths that started right next to my house. How lovely were the hills at every season, whether in the lush springtime or the early autumn when the different kinds of thistle bloomed with violet puffs out of the thorny head of the plant.

It was after the false peace ushered in by the Oslo Accord of 1995 that economic development, held back for many years by Israeli-imposed restrictions, began to be fostered and financed by EU and US aid programmes. This was coupled with law reform programmes aimed at the commodification of real estate, making it possible to market apartments in a building rather than own them communally. It was a similar process to that which the British initiated in Palestine during the Mandate in order to facilitate the sale of Palestinian land to the Zionists. The change in the law made it possible for investors to build high-rise blocks and sell the individual flats. With the scarcity of land available for Palestinians, inappropriately high buildings were piled up on the hills with little space in between. Every plot had to be exploited to the maximum to make up for the high price paid to acquire it. Houses with gardens became a luxury which only a few could afford. Every city needs open green areas, breathing spaces between the dense construction. Our city cannot have those because the land left for its development and expansion is restricted. The Jewish settlements all around have the larger share of land. The settlement of Ma'ale Adumim, east of Jerusalem, sits on an area larger than Tel Aviv. They have vast swathes in which to establish green open spaces, whereas we in Ramallah have to live in a confined space. On Fridays the nearby hills, which lie in what is called Area C under Israeli jurisdiction, where building is not allowed, fill up with families taking their grills and sitting under the olive trees to enjoy the outdoors. The rules imposed by Israel prevent us from turning these into proper parks.

The area where I lived at the edge of town, which used to be pastoral, has been invaded by developments and become a busy, crowded place. The end of the street where the meandering path once began has become a crossroads, connecting roads that extend in every direction. At all times of day and night innumerable cars pass by my old one-storey, semi-detached house, heading to the various tall buildings all around it. So many roads have been opened through the once-lovely hills. The terraces and olive trees are gone. The attractive hills on the periphery, where it used to be possible to ramble, have become blocked by landslides of rubble from the nearby construction work. My old stone house by the fig tree, once surrounded by low drystone walls and situated in a veritable natural garden of rolling hills criss-crossed by ancient paths that one could take at will and walk all the way to the surrounding villages, has become confined, surrounded by tall buildings on all sides.

Even before the problem became endemic I could see where we were heading. I knew how much the city would benefit from leaving one of the hillsides green with the stone terracing intact, yet I realised it would be futile to lobby for this. The obstacles were too many. The price of land was prohibitive. Instead I wrote and lamented the vanishing of the unique landscape. The activist in me was turned into the writer.

And now we live in a crowded city where the beauty and innocence all around us have been destroyed. In the past it did not matter that there were no designated green areas in Ramallah, situated as it was in a large natural garden of its own. But now that the surrounding hills have been built upon, when Ramallah desperately needs those open areas, the land is not available.

I remember standing, not long ago, on Mount Scopus in Jerusalem and seeing how the Israeli authorities were not leaving any land for the Palestinians of Jerusalem, taking what they could and changing the status of what they couldn't into green areas, simply so that the Palestinians would be unable

to use them. I consoled myself by thinking that this injustice couldn't possibly last. As I played the role of incorrigible optimist despite all the dreadful examples of oppression I saw around me, I could sense a look of extreme sadness descending on my face, which became contorted with pain even as it strove to hide behind that expression of confidence and hope I was committed to preserve. Perhaps both faces were false.

After I got married in 1988 I left Helen's house, hauling with me box after box full of copies of my journals and published writings produced over the years that I'd spent there. When I think of the massive amount of writing I did about the legal and human rights aspects of the occupation and how little difference it made, I wonder whether I wasted a large part of my life on a useless activity. To warn? But whom? I was still naïve enough to believe that the world was ruled by a benevolent father who would ultimately come to our assistance and save us if only he knew. My father died and the world has abandoned us. And I've had to accept this. That impish look on my face is long gone.

As I continued looking at my former house with the overgrown shrubs and trees surrounding it, a more worrisome thought came to me and I found myself asking: could it be that I have lived a mock existence of words, led a false paper life? And yet what gave meaning and weight to the various periods of my life was the writing I did. Could writing, then, have been the home I was always searching for?

I do not begrudge my time as an activist. How can I? It was what gave meaning to my life then, what gave me hope, what saved me from getting depressed and giving up. It allowed me to stand up and be counted. It helped make me who I am. Was it not worth it for that? And yet as I pursued my triple profession as a lawyer, writer and human rights activist, I became arrogant and vain, and this had complicated my relationship with my father.

Neither my father nor my mother ever visited me here. Perhaps they were ashamed of the conditions I was living in, perhaps they wanted to respect my privacy. But once, before I was due to travel to the US for another of those human rights conferences, my father drove over and honked. I went out to see who it was. He had brought me some *baraziq* (very thin, crisp, salty sesame cakes) from Jerusalem. He knew how much I liked these. They always reminded me of happy times spent with my grandmother in the garden at the Grand Hotel. It was a generous gesture on his part, but rather than use the opportunity of his being here without my mother to invite him in and perhaps have a man-to-man conversation, I took his present, thanked him and bid him farewell.

Shortly after, while I was away, I learned of his murder. That brief encounter was one of my last with my father.

Five

From my old house I walked back to Tireh Road. The cafés at this end of the street have become extremely popular and are visited by fashionably dressed young women driving expensive cars who stop to smoke a *nergila*. At the weekend young men come in Bermuda shorts and slippers to spend their mornings sipping espresso and smoking.

In the past, men in Ramallah never wore shorts in public. In the last few years there has been a sea change in the appearance of people in the streets. Many more women cover their hair and young men now sport fancy punk styles with the sides shaved and puffy hair on top. When you pass them they emit a strong smell of perfume. In the past, men and women in the street smelled natural, in the summer with the stink of perspiration. Now, with the proliferation of cheap perfumes and a dispensation from the imams that the Prophet Muhammad liked fragrance and wore it, this has changed. The people I saw going to cafés have lived all their life under occupation. There have already been two generations since it began in 1967.

On one side of the street a café offered alcohol and

no *nergila*. It was full of women with attractive flowing hair. On the other side there was *nergila* but no alcohol. It was full of mainly women in scarves, representing the division in Palestinian society in Ramallah. Both are very popular and always busy. You could smell and see the heavy scented smoke as you passed by.

I decided to turn left and take the side street named after Labib Hishmeh in appreciation of his participation in the scout movement. I wanted to have a look at the hills to the east even though it meant going down and then having to walk up again. Like many other streets in Ramallah, this one was named after a member of an old local family, most of whose members no longer live here. The dead man and his descendants have been in the US for decades. It's as though the original inhabitants, having left the city, now want to be remembered by lobbying for streets to be named after deceased family members like a rare, extinct species.

At the corner of the slope, just before I began climbing up Damascus Road, I noticed that the recently opened eastward street is called Ayn Louzeh after the spring that used to be there before the area was developed. The large water-loving eucalyptus trees lining both sides of the road are presumably drawing on the underground spring below. Who now would remember how lovely this area used to be, with that old ruin of a house by the spring with almond trees that bloomed in February, a nearby cave and, in April, fields of yellow mallow growing on one terrace and pyramid orchids on another?

When I reached halfway up the road that would take me back to Main Street, I passed one of the old Ramallah houses built seventy years ago. It was occupied by a family of limited means. All the windows and doors were open and I could hear loud exuberant Arabic music blaring out from the house. Dirty water was draining into the street. I could not see the woman inside the house, but I could sense her determined energy as she swept everything away and for the first time I understood what she must be feeling. The evening before the house would have been full of people, her husband, children and their friends. They all ate and the men smoked. It is the habit of some men here not to care about what gets spilled. She must have sat there deferentially in the small space allotted to her that would only have dwindled as the number and gender of the guests increased. She could see food being spilled and cigarette butts extinguished underfoot. But this morning it was all hers. The children and the men were out. Now she was mistress of the whole space. It was her chance to assert her dominion, to sweep away all remnants of their presence, all evidence of their offensive practices. She was doing it in the most efficient manner by splashing water, huge bucket-loads of it, over the entire tiled floor. The water would run everywhere, underneath the beds, chairs and tables, into corners and over the balcony, leaving no spot in the house untouched, uncleansed. All the ash, food, cigarette butts, scraps of paper and whatever was left behind by those careless men who never have to pick up anything after themselves would be swept out of the house and into the street, where it belonged. She would be in flip-flops, with the ends of her trousers rolled up. Could she be swaying to the music as she waged her battle with the water to drive it out of the house? The sounds reverberating in the empty house are her choice of music. There is no one to object that it is too cold to have the windows open. Running around, she does not feel the morning chill. All the furniture has been moved to allow her to clean underneath and behind it; the throws, covers and floor mats are all shaken clean. Nothing is left where it had been the night before, when everyone behaved as they wished, while she kept to her corner, watching without comment or objection.

The dirt and murky water streaked with soapsuds drained

into the street. As I passed by I was assaulted by its fusty smell. I stepped aside just in time to avoid being splashed as it sidled down the street with its clusters of hair and scraps of food.

As I stood watching this, I thought of how again and again our larger houses, our city and our countryside have been defiled by the invading Israeli army, but it was always left to us to clean up the mess. The first time was in 1967, when there was minimal destruction to property. Then in 2002 the Israeli army invaded again, in the process devastating so many homes and offices. After the invasion a slogan appeared saying, 'Tomorrow is a better day and like a phoenix we shall rise again.' Compared to where we were then and where we are now, this was an apt metaphor to use.

At the top of the street I turn left. On the corner there used to be an attractive old house which was demolished in 1982. In its place now stands a three-storey building containing box-like flats. I remember our efforts to save that old building, another battle we lost. Opposite, Yasser Arafat's brother Fathi established what he called a heritage shop, selling Palestine cross-stitch embroidered cushions and other items in the Palestinian colours. He also built a hotel run by the Palestinian Red Cross Society on the football pitch serving the Amari Camp School and the only open space near the crowded refugee camp. The returning leaders of our national movement were compensating for losing the battle for the land with this celebration of heritage, while ensuring the financial viability of Fatah, the largest political group.

Coming down the street I saw Fadda, whose name means silver, the long-term domestic helper of the former mayor of Ramallah, who had been appointed by Israel after the start of the occupation. She greeted me furtively, looking round as though she did not want anyone to see that she was talking to me. She was all eyes, fully aware of everything around her, and yet she put on a coy, bashful look, her shield against the world. She made me think of an opinion piece I had read by a *Times* columnist in 1973 when I was a law student in London. The writer was remembering his nanny and wondering what she would have achieved had she had the educational opportunities that the British welfare system now provides for those with limited means. Had Fadda been given the opportunity, she would have made something of herself; instead all her life had been spent cleaning a house that was not her own. Our dream when we worked in solidarity during the first Intifada was that we would help create an egalitarian society where everyone, including people like Fadda, would get the opportunity to shine.

Further up the road I saw two other women. One, wearing a traditional embroidered dress, was sitting on the ledge by the pavement fingering her worry beads. She was tall and had the graceful body of women from the Hebron region in the south of the West Bank. She had great presence and offered friendly greetings to every passer-by, many of whom stopped to talk to her. She lived in a cavernous one-room house built in 1911 below street level, one of those houses in Ramallah's old city that had escaped demolition. The other, in modern dress, lived in a windowless ground-floor room in an attractive old Ramallah house long abandoned by its owners, who were living in the US. It had a thick wooden door that squeaked open directly on to the pavement. The two women never spoke to each other, nor did they seem to acknowledge each other's existence. The woman with modern dress looked disgruntled, fed up with the world, as she sat in the frame of the open door on a low wicker chair. Her feet rested on the lower panel of the open blue-grey door with the big wrought-iron key of the old Ramallah houses. She was wearing a burgundy sweater and a grey skirt. Underneath her raised feet, almost covered by her skirt, a grey and black cat sat on its haunches, content as only cats can be, looking at

passers-by from the comfort and security of this woman's skirt. The woman was sewing a cross-stitch cushion cover using black and red threads. She did this for a wage. She was so intent on her work that she did not look up. Her hair was shoulder-length and grey. She lived all alone, her children having emigrated to the US. Upstairs the house was deserted. Most likely the owners were waiting for the old tenant to die or to leave, so they could demolish the house and sell up for the astronomical price that land near the centre now fetches.

Further along I came to the first traffic lights. A line of cars waited for the sombre face painted on the red light to be replaced by the smiley face painted on the green light. Once again I felt so fortunate to be walking rather than driving. I noticed a Palestinian flag unceremoniously fluttering in the air. Such a sight is no longer momentous. This practice is now ubiquitous. It is one of the few victories that was won with the Oslo deal. In the past flying the flag constituted a dangerous heroic deed that could cost lives. Now there is neither honour nor gratification in watching it flutter over the city of our confinement. Israel doesn't care what symbols of state Palestinians exhibit. It continues to do what it can to prevent one from materialising on the ground.

At the corner a new building was going up. A few weeks earlier I was in a shared taxi and we passed this construction site where the last of the city's woodcutters used to be. I was chatting with the taxi driver and mentioned that I hoped this new building would not be so close to the blind corner that the road could not be widened. Evidently this was not what was happening. Even as I said this I was angered at how lacking in public spirit the owner was. In a matter-of-fact way, devoid of malice or anger, the taxi driver said, *'Sahibha wasel* [its owner has connections]. Even when he was pouring cement the police would block the whole street.' I was struck by how calmly he said this and how he was willing to accept such discrimination. For him *wasel* was a fact of life that he was reconciled to, could do nothing about and must simply accept. In his driving he was also accepting, not allowing himself to get worked up by all the terrible drivers. If he did he would not be able to complete the day without collapsing.

Beyond the traffic lights I crossed the street to look at a garden I admire. It belongs to a woman who lives in humble circumstances in one of the old Ramallah houses built in 1927. It has a small space in front, below street level, which gets little sun and yet she has managed to keep beds of decorative plants and a few herbs. You can always tell when a garden is the product of a hired gardener or the loving hands of the owner. I much prefer gardens with a personal touch like this one.

In front was an ugly, bulky building in which the Arab Bank has its headquarters, built where the Ramallah bus terminal used to be. Until 1994 this was an open space in the centre of the old city, providing somewhere to breathe in the crowded area. I'm told there used to be a spring here. It is where we were instructed to gather in 1991 during the First Gulf War for the distribution of gas masks. We were certain that without these we were doomed to die of the poison gas Saddam Hussein was supposed to possess. We all enthusiastically heeded the call, but of course the Israeli military failed to provide them. A frightening time.

It is regrettable that this area was not kept as an open space. But in the chaos that ensued during the transition period just before the Palestinian Authority began taking responsibility for civilian affairs from the Israeli military, a permit to build was issued and the area changed forever. To the left of the unsightly building was the old *hisba* (vegetable market), before it was moved to Ramallah's sister town of Al Bireh.

I remember walking to the Al Bireh *hisba* when the curfew

was lifted after the First Gulf War. I wanted so much to hear 'the busy hum of men' and knew I would find it there. How I yearned after our long and anxious confinement to be around people. In the course of my ordeal during the war I had also forgotten what a feast for the senses, an olfactory chorus, it was to walk through the spice market leading to the *hisba*. There were strong aromas of chamomile, sage and mint from the numerous herb, spice and dried-fruit shops lining the street. The pavement was crammed with sacks of brown dried figs, raisins, black carob beans (those long horn-like pods that remind one of biblical times) and white solid yoghurt balls. One of the shops was grinding thyme leaves and their dry, piercing smell, which is captured by the front of the nose, saturated the air. This was followed by the deeper, more rounded smell of sesame seeds being roasted and the mouth-watering, soothing smell of baked bread that strikes deep at the stomach. Further on was the rakish smell of grilled chickens turning on spits and of *shawarma* sizzling as the fat dropped from the slices of meat on the spike, with the fire blazing behind. And then there were the ubiquitous falafel stands, where the round brown patties were cooked in boiling sesame oil with its pungent smell that assaulted you full in the face.

And it remains as it was then. In Al Bireh this double chorus of smells and sounds remains unaltered. But the area of the old Ramallah *hisba*, south of where I was walking, which used to be the hub of resistance to the occupation, has now become unrecognisably gentrified, with pavement cafés that often leave no room for pedestrians to pass, pizza and hamburger places with foreign-sounding names, and an active nightlife. It also has become a centre for a number of cultural and musical institutions. One of these is Al Kamandjati, which has been influential since its establishment in 2002 in popularising both Arabic and Western classical music, and offering music lessons, especially to deprived children from refugee camps. It is run by Ramzi Aburedwan, himself from Amari camp. It operates out of a renovated building not far from the old Ramallah municipal building now used as a one-stop-shop facility, where it's possible to check on and pay all municipal and other taxes in the same place.

As I passed this municipal one-stop shop I remembered the Western expert sent after the Oslo Accords to help the Palestinian Authority develop modern methods. How he went on and on about the possibility of gathering in one place all the transactions for payments, and how confused the official was as he tried to understand what this 'expert' was talking about, using English which he could barely understand. When he finally got it, he couldn't stop saying, 'Yes, yes, it is good, one-stop shop, one-stop shop.'

In recent years Ramallah has acquired three music academies. In February 1967 my father and a number of other music lovers worked on plans to establish the first. The occupation put a stop to their efforts. It was many decades later that their dream materialised. Of the twenty-eight founding members, only six have remained in Palestine; the rest have either emigrated or died. As well as the music academies, there are a number of concert halls where world-famous musicians perform. An audience appreciative of classical music has been cultivated.

In the early 1950s many of the old city houses were rented to country people who came to Ramallah from the Hebron region's impoverished villages, such as Sair and Thahrieh, seeking work. The previous owners of these houses had emigrated to the US. With the rent-control law in force, tenants were unwilling to move. This remained the case until their situation improved once work in Israel became an option and they left to live in better housing. This was when wholesale renovation could begin and now only a scattering of families continue to inhabit the old houses built early in the last century. As I walk along the city's familiar streets, passing its monuments, murals and museums, I try to get to grips with what has become of it after half a century of occupation.

Twenty-five years after the establishment of the Palestinian Authority few opportunities for work have been found for those labouring away in Israel, many of whom are employed in building the illegal Israeli settlements. Their numbers continue to rise. Their morning begins at two-thirty. They have to drive to the checkpoints, where they are made to wait for hours before they're allowed through on foot. Only then do they proceed to their place of work in Israel or to the Jewish settlements, returning exhausted in the late afternoon. They are the unseen who suffer in silence, glad to find work in Israel or at the settlements, however harsh and humiliating the conditions. Once, when I was returning from travel early in the morning, I saw a number of them crossing the highway to smuggle themselves into Israel. The car lights reflected on their white shirts as though a flock of birds had flown across. By the time I started my walk this morning, none could be seen. They were all already at work.

For the past week, every time I've walked to the office I've noticed an old man with a long necktie sitting near the kerb, at the same corner by the pavement, looking wistful as if bidding farewell to the scene before his eyes. And he was there again today, in the same place and with the same pose. He was frail, with quick, sudden movements which were then followed by moments of long repose. Who was he? A man who was dying or an expat who was visiting after a long absence and possibly for the last time? He wore a red and black waistcoat and always started the day by sitting near the kerb, his nose almost touching his long narrow chin, his mouth firmly closed, his eyes looking dreamily into the distance. Both his hands rested on the crook of his smooth, amber-coloured wooden cane. Something about him intrigued me, sitting as he did bent over, reflecting on his life as he scrutinised every passer-by. Then I saw him lift one of his hands, hold it up to support his long chin, which was framed by two of his fingers, and rest his elbow on the crook of his staff. He seemed to keep this pose for a long time. I found myself observing him with fascination, worried that one day I might end up like him, posing at street corners in Ramallah, directing my gaze to the horizon in a long vacant stare.

Looking at him made me wonder what it takes to remain human in a place so buffeted by aggression, dominated by the struggle for survival. How is it possible to avoid resorting to anger and utter hatred, and at the same time guard against becoming insular and insensitive? There is no telling how much longer this occupation will last. Both of my parents' lives ended before they saw a resolution of the struggle. And mine may as well. I've always had to conserve my energies and prepare for survival under these harsh and distressing conditions for an indeterminate length of time. But I know from my experience in the first Intifada that days lost cannot be compensated for. I am no longer young. I don't feel I have limitless time during which I will remain physically well. I don't want to end up feeling embittered, standing on a street corner like that old man, with a sense that my life has been lost, dissipated.

But no! I will not turn into a withered old man like this mysterious person manning street corners, or like those other old men, so common here, who rant in broken voices about what they did in their youth for the cause and how unappreciated they were and how things would have turned out differently if only the politicians had listened to them. I will live a fulfilled life. Each year will be better than the one that preceded it. If the practice of law is no longer going to be rewarding, then

66

I will move on to some other pursuit. This man is a warning of what I could become.

My musings were interrupted by the sight of Abu Muhammad, who is probably in his fifties. He was on his way to our neighbourhood, where he often finds work cleaning the pavements. Close to his chest, like a handbag, he held a white bucket in which was a black plastic bag, and balanced on his shoulder was his long broom. A rake with the tines up was used as a cane that he made look like a sceptre. He walked unevenly between the cars, avoiding the pavement. For many years now he has been coming over to seek work. He would make his presence known from a distance by singing. Then he would ring the bell. 'Do you need your pavement cleaned this morning?' he would ask politely. And if I said, 'Not today,' he would thank me and leave.

He takes the bus from one of the downtrodden, impoverished villages northwest of Ramallah which has no pavements, then he walks from the centre of the city heading north to Tireh, where the well-off families live. After leaving my door, he proceeds to one of the neighbours, announcing his presence by his singing. When the singing stops I realise he has secured a job for the day.

I'm comforted to know that he has started covering his bald head with a cap to protect his scalp from the sun. I could see a worryingly large lump protruding from the back of his head and it had been increasing in size since he began coming over to look for work five years ago. Several times he's asked me, 'They say America is down there by the roundabout, down this hill. Is it true?' He laughs and shakes his shoulders, as if he's enjoying his own joke.

One day when I was returning home for lunch he had almost finished sweeping the neighbours' pavement, doing his usual meticulous job, filling his bucket with rubbish and plucking out the weeds growing between the kerb and the tarmac and dumping them all in the field over the road, only for the wind to eventually spread them back again on the pavement.

'Where have you been?' he asks.

'Out,' I say.

'In America?'

'Yes, in America.'

'I was once there, you know?'

'Who took you there?'

'Vera.' (Vera Tamari is the artist who lives in a house next to ours.)

'Why did she take you to America?'

'Why? To show me. She took me in her car and we went to the hill over there and stopped the car and I looked down.'

'And what did you see?'

'All kinds of fantastic things. I saw big trees and big houses. Everything so big and the pavements so wide and clean. They don't need me there. The walls were high, but I could see from where we stood up on the hill blue water. Yes, they say it's the ocean. I saw the ocean. Vera showed it to me!'

I remain silent, so he continues.

'They say in America you find gold on the pavements. But I couldn't get down because of the growling dogs. I don't know if it was true about the gold, but I saw America.'

'And how did you find it?' I asked.

'Amazing.'

He chuckles. I cannot tell whether he is giggling in self-mockery or laughing at my incredulity, or at the absurdity of the inequity of our world.

'Bring me a wife from America,' he sings. 'I want a blonde one. Yes, I want to marry her.' Then, as he walks away, he asks, 'They say in America they put the dollars in burlap bags. Is it true?'

The kindly man who took every rejection of an offer to work so politely, with such tolerance and grace, was walking in his uncertain way down the street towards Tireh Road as I stood watching him from behind.

Not far from where I was standing a young man of eighteen, Ayman Ratib Jabarin, was killed by Israeli soldiers on 22 June 2006, during the tail end of the second Intifada. There was a plaque commemorating the spot and a street named after him. I wondered whether he was a grandson of one of the families who came to Ramallah from Sair, near Hebron, the family who owned a bakery nearby. I crossed the street to check whether it was still there. I passed through the narrow one-way lane between the walls of the two buildings on either side, hardly metres apart, remnants of old Ramallah. The original city, said to have been established in the mid-1550s, consisted of eight clans, each living in its own *hara* (quarter). The one I was entering was where the Yousef *hamoula* (extended family or clan) lived. Just around the corner the bakery made its presence known by the strong comforting smell of freshly baked bread. I popped my head in. It was just as I remembered it, with cobwebs on the arched ceiling and wooden paddles to put the bread in the oven and take it out again. Only they no longer baked the flat bread for the women who brought dough they prepared at home. Now they made the round sesame cakes with the hollow centre that are very popular and sold uptown on the busy streets of Ramallah.

Walking through the narrow lane, I recalled how, as I was growing up, we made our own dough and took it to this same bakery for baking. My mother's helper, Adeeba, would have prepared the yeast days before, feeding it with water and flour until it became active, bubbly and billowy. She would use some of it to mix with the flour and water, keeping the rest for the next session. She would dig the knuckles of her long, strong

hands in the dough and knead it. Then she would pat the pliable mass that felt almost alive, taming it into one big soft ball that she covered with a heavy cloth and slipped under the couch in the sitting room. Next morning she would remove the cover and check that the dough had risen. We called this sourdough bread *samoune*. She would roll up a white cotton sash into a circle which she placed on her head and gently lift the big dish containing the dough on to it, then walk in a slow, stately manner to the bakery at the corner, down from the house of the bad boys who often came out to play in the street without their underwear. I would walk down with her, holding her hand.

Usually there were many other women already at the bakery, all with dough ready or, for the more energetic, the lunch dish of chicken or vegetables that they wanted to go in the oven. They would talk together as they busily separated the dough into small fist-sized balls, which they placed on the flat straw tray to be picked up by the baker. Meanwhile I examined the intricate spirals of cobwebs in the arched domes of this old bakery. The walls were blackened all the way up to the ceiling. Saah, the baker, wore short sleeves that showed his muscular arms. He was silent as he placed the round pieces of dough on his paddles. If the customer's order was for *samoune* bread, he kept the dough as one lump; if they wanted *wardi* he flattened it, beat it lightly with his nimble fingers and then dug all ten fingers up and down to make holes in the dough, after which he quickly hurled it into the fire. As soon as this was done he pulled out the earlier load of bread, now steaming hot, from inside the oven. I watched with fascination, my face glowing in the heat from the open hearth, wondering how it was that the wooden paddle that was shoved in and out of the oven did not catch fire. I had to back up as the hot bread was hurled on to Adeeba's straw tray while she stood waiting. She would juggle it up and down to cool it, then arrange one piece next to another in tidy rows. After she'd received the lot, she would cover the hot bread with a cloth, mount it on her head, take my hand and set off again. And so we'd saunter back to the house: Adeeba, tall and straight as a rod, with her dignified pace, and me, short and with my head bent, surveying the ground, lost in my own private world as I munched on a crust of the hot bread, my favourite food.

I could smell the freshly baked sesame cakes as I passed the old bakery. But I did not consider buying any. It has been almost two years now since I've eaten any wheat bread. Now I can only enjoy the smell.

1. My parents, Aziz and Wedad, with their first born, Siham, in Jaffa.

2. Me, standing by the gate of our first house in Ramallah, with the empty hills in the background.

3. With my sister Samar and our helper Adeeba
in the *saha* (yard) of our first house.

4. My father is holding my younger brother Samer during a
Christmas party at our first house; to his left is my older sister
Siham and next to her my mother. Leaning forward, next to Santa,
is my sister Samar whose birthday is on 21 December, so she's
blowing out the candles of her birthday cake. I'm standing next
to her, with her friends who are attending her birthday party.

5. A New Year party, with dancing.

6. A competition at the dancing rink of the
Grand Hotel in which I participated.

7. My grandmother Julia.

8. The Shehadeh family preparing for an outing in the mid fifties, before my brother Samer was born.

9. With my parents in their home, circa 1967.

10. My parents at their sun balcony in the early eighties.

Six

From the bakery I walked up through the old city, looking at all the changes taking place. Unlike the area behind the massive Arab Bank building that I had passed earlier, this part has retained more of its old flavour, with narrow winding alleys and some of the traditional homes still standing. These were designed to have two floors, the lower one reserved for the animals while the family slept above. They had thick walls and solid wooden doors, now worn with age and imbued with recollections over many decades of the generations of families who lived there. The doors had huge wrought-iron keys that could not be copied and were much more effective than the Israeli-made multi-lock doors, so undifferentiated and characterless. But the keys were bulky and heavy, indicating that the owners of these homes rarely ever left them without someone staying behind.

I was surprised there were no children playing in the streets. This was so unlike the way it used to be when I was growing up here. Abu Abid's obdurate and often-abused mule that pulled the cart delivering kerosene for cooking and heating used to leave many blobs of dung on the street. The children didn't have to worry much about passing cars then. One would pass every few hours and the local bus made the rounds twice a day, in the morning and the afternoon. Now the streets are full of speeding vehicles and children sit at their computers or with their smartphones, playing electronic games and growing obese. There are no mule-drawn carts left in Ramallah, so no dung either. But domestic dogs can be seen, being walked by proud owners showing them off. Pets have finally arrived in Ramallah.

In the old city I knew as a child nothing was wasted. Families could not afford, nor would they ever consider wasting the money, to buy toys for their children. Children made their own toys from pieces of junk. Old wires from discarded electric cables were turned into small carts that could be driven and turned around with a handle, reminiscent of minimalist art objects. Balls were made from string. Girls made dolls from rags. Children used their imagination and skill to entertain themselves. A popular toy was made from rolled-up wire turned into a hoop and driven with a stick. As it gathered speed, the boys would run to keep up with it. The five-year-old son of a neighbour of ours ran into one of the occasional cars coming down the street and was killed.

Most of the men and women passing through the streets of the old city wore traditional Palestinian village dress. For the women it was the colourful *toub* with hand-stitched patterns and colours peculiar to Ramallah, red and black, usually with a sash and a headdress festooned with old Ottoman coins. The men wore the *serwal*, a long grey garment resembling the shalwar kameez worn by Pakistani men, with faint black stripes and a thick colourful cloth belt. In winter they wrapped themselves with a loose overgarment we called *abayah* (cloak). This attire did not distinguish between people on religious grounds. Now those who still wear such clothes are a rare sight. When talk of immigration to the US was being discussed, one old relative of mine wearing a *toub* joked that if she ended up going to America she would have to wear a bra. She thought this was hilarious and with her gnarled old hands lifted her drooping breasts to indicate how it would be, laughing as she did so.

It was then the custom, as it remains for some in Ramallah, to visit the eldest member of the extended family, who is considered its head, on feast days. My father was in that position, which meant that rather than go out and enjoy ourselves on such days, our house filled up with visitors, some of whom came only on these occasions, and my mother had to serve the traditional feast pastries and brew Turkish coffee for all of them. Every year she would complain to my father, who felt he had to tolerate the practice. Then one feast day she announced that it had to stop. She convinced my father to dissuade everyone from coming and they stopped showing up. My mother always managed to get her way. Though I thought, as I was growing up, that it was the other way round.

Thinking about the still-empty plot where my father had planned to build a house, I remember that when I was a child, after the 1948 Nakba (catastrophe), refugees from Lifta had taken possession of the empty house across the street from ours, which was owned by a woman who was in the US. They had brought cows from their village and put them on that empty plot. I wonder now how my mother must have felt about ending up living next to a cowshed after leaving her glamorous life in the affluent and cultured city of Jaffa, where her husband had a flourishing law practice. They had just moved into their exquisitely furnished new flat when they were forced out of the city, along with some three-quarters of a million Palestinians, in what came to be known as the Nakba. Surely it must have made her feel she had fallen from grace. Where once she had been the daughter of an affluent judge living in a cosmopolitan city, she was now across the street from the smelly cows of the *Lafatawis* (people of Lifta).

The more sordid the surroundings, the more tenaciously my mother held on to her dreams and gave free rein to her imagination. This was especially strong during the Christmas season, when she managed to create an exciting holiday atmosphere, dressing up as Father Christmas and going round to all the terrified youngsters at the Christmas party she hosted in our house, changing her voice and taking our trembling hands in her red-gloved hand to hop around and sing together. Then, after removing her disguise, she would come back to the throng, expressing her sorrow that she had missed the fun, convincing us that it was not she who had been behind the mask.

She would tell me bedtime stories about queens living in luxury and I imagined her to be one. Outside was the harsh material world and under the warm eiderdown into which I tucked myself next to her I heard magical tales of happy kings, queens and princes living in sumptuous palaces. How enraptured I was by that imaginary world. I promised my mother that when I grew older, wherever I happened to be at Christmas, I would always travel home to be with her.

Working my way through the narrow lanes of the old city, I discover that a number of the old houses I had known have been demolished and replaced by modern buildings. I continue on towards the old house where I spent the first fourteen years of my life, stopping to check the garden of Nahida Jaber, now an octogenarian, on the way. Unlike her late husband, Nahida has always been resourceful and had a well-ordered spirit, allowing her to feel perfectly satisfied with her own company and able to retire into her own being. She rarely leaves the house. She gardens, reads and enjoys her extended family of children, grandchildren and great-grandchildren and their spouses, for whom she often cooks. Her garden is her world and is by far the best in the city.

As I looked over the wall, I thought the garden looked

glorious. No ostentation here and none of the unsightly palm trees that now seem to be a must in all new gardens. The front garden was awash with colour, annuals of different sorts competing with each other to dazzle. On every step of the stairway leading up to the front door was a plant pot full of flowering geraniums. On the side in a shady alcove there were pots brimming with fuchsias, which I've always found difficult to cultivate in Ramallah because of the dry heat. Nahida's success was astounding. So many passers-by stop to photograph the garden that the family had placed a 'No Photography' sign by the gate.

In 1989 the Israeli military had ordered that the house, which was originally built in 1941, be demolished. Nader, one of Nahida's sons, had been involved in an armed operation against Israel, an act punishable by the demolition of the house of the perpetrator's family. Nader had managed to narrowly avoid capture by leaving the country and so his family's home was threatened instead. Al Haq, the human rights organisation affiliated with the International Commission of Jurists which I had helped establish and was directing then, waged a massive campaign to halt this disproportionate response and succeeded in getting the military to amend the order and demolish only the studio flat on the third floor of the three-storey building where Nader was living. I remember how anxious this made Ramzi, Nader's father, who feared that the explosion would render the whole house uninhabitable. But it didn't. Severe as the Israeli military are, they make precise calculations. The rest of the house survived and, after the signing of the Oslo Accords, Nader's brothers rebuilt the demolished floor. Nonetheless, more than a quarter of a century has passed since this happened and Nader now lives abroad. He is still not allowed to return home; even when his father died, he could not attend the funeral.

On reaching our old house on Dar Yousef Street, I was pleased to see again the Syrian pines which my grandmother had planted when the house was built in the 1930s. They were as towering and straggly as they had always been, shading both the house and the garden. A small house intended for summer use, it was open to the northwest, from where the wind blew, making it difficult to heat in winter. After my family were forced out of Jaffa in April 1948 this became our permanent home. We lived downstairs and my grandmother lived upstairs alone. She would often spend the morning on the balcony with its three arches, seated in one of her green wicker chairs.

Our *hara* was very mixed. Nearby lived Nazli, the Armenian midwife, and next door there was a Circassian family. The father was a short, frail man with a long, thin nose and a small face dominated by large ears. He often played on his accordion lively music with a strong beat that to us sounded like Russian tunes. Originally from a region in the north Caucasus, his people had fled from persecution in the late nineteenth century and ended up in Syria and Jordan. They were Muslims who retained their own language and traditions. Many fought with the Jordanian army and were loyal to the regime. We hardly ever spoke to the man we referred to as the *Sharkasi* (Circassian), but he was always spying on us to find out who was visiting our house. When my father was arrested for sheltering his communist friend Ibrahim Bakr, an incorrigible political activist who was later deported by Israel after the beginning of the occupation and became a prominent lawyer in Amman, we found out that it was the *Sharkasi* who had informed on us to the Jordanian police. Years later, upon Bakr's release, I remember this stout man with a deep voice, whom I admired for his fortitude and courage, seating me next to him and tenderly telling me of a distant freer world, asking whether I knew of the existence of the vast expanding universe populated by innumerable stars and unexplored horizons. With his words and the use of his long fingers, he helped me imagine the spacious firmament on high. I listened with fascination, totally mesmerised. It was the first time that I was taken away in my imagination beyond the small but enchanting world I inhabited.

The Circassian family had a young son, a loner who kept himself to himself and did not associate with the other children in our *hara*. When he was five, they had a celebration which they said was a circumcision. I did not go, but others did. For days before it was due to take place, everyone pointed at the boy and said he was going to be circumcised, which seemed to embarrass him. He also looked worried, and the snot that had run from his small nose and stopped at his upper lip looked like it was frozen there. He seemed too distracted to wipe it away. Then, after it was over, he came out on to the street wearing a white robe because, they said, his penis was tied up and he could not be in trousers. And then that family left. Next, Zaki Hussary, a refugee from Lydda (now called Lod, in Israel), and his wife, Eileen, who were forced out of their city at gunpoint in July 1948, leaving everything behind, moved in. This significantly increased the number of refugees living in Ramallah. According to the 1953 census, out of a population of 13,500 people in the city 8,500 were refugees.

Zaki and Eileen had no children. They adopted one of their nephews, who years later told me how envious he was of us at Christmas because we got so many presents. One time my sister Siham sent him a present and he has never forgotten her kind gesture, remaining eternally grateful. Zaki, who was a truck driver, insisted that Eileen bake fresh bread every day. He worked hard and lived in penury; eating fresh bread was one of the few luxuries he insisted on. There was another family, also refugees from Lydda, who lived in the stairwell in the house across the street from ours. Every one of their eight children slept on a different step. This family has now managed very well and their grandson drives a Mercedes.

Ramallah's economy was weak and could not provide full employment for its inhabitants. By the late 1950s more and more people were emigrating. There was an obese woman called Najla whom, because of her size, we always called Najla Al Bansa (fat Najla). She sold sweets which she kept in glass jars. She had a well-marked small chin that was sweaty and I used to think it looked funny, situated as it was among the folds of fat on her large face. But above that chin she had a serious, lugubrious face that belied the cute chin. We would keenly knock on her metal door. The minute she opened it we would be confronted by the musty odour of her house. One day we went to buy sweets and banged on her door but no one answered. We banged harder and the wall began to collapse. We scrambled over into the downed metal walls and saw that there was nothing left, none of the jars, none of the furniture, just the metal sheets spread on the ground. Najla Al Bansa had joined the ranks of those who went in search of a new life in America.

My family considered emigrating only once, when the Jordanian authorities' harassment of my father became intolerable. But then my parents decided against it. Prior to 1967 my mother glorified Jaffa and her father the judge, how he knew what was going to happen to their city and how once they left they would never see their house again. Then, after the '67 war, my father fantasised about a new era of peace with Israel with a Palestinian state next to it, and cooperation between the two nations in which he would play a part. He strongly believed that it would happen if his advice was heeded. But it did not come to fruition. I, of course, being a dutiful son, continued to believe that it would.

As a child on summer mornings I would be passed like a parcel over the wire fence that separated our house from the neighbours'. 'Giv'm to me, giv'm to me,' my aunt and our neighbour Wadia would say, and I would be handed over. Wadia's father was a brilliant doctor who had been employed as the private physician of the Ottoman Sultan in Istanbul. Her husband, Salem Ghannam, ate eggs with yoghurt, which everyone thought was odd. I later realised this was a Turkish recipe that he must have learned from his mother-in-law. Wadia would hug and kiss me with a sucking sound and give me biscuits dipped in coffee. I liked this very much. When *Tata* came to claim me back, Wadia would declare, *'Hatha husti'* (he's mine). Perhaps for her I temporarily replaced the son who had left and was never close.

Wadia had a substantial behind and was always burdened with problems. She wore her dressing gown all day. When she came to visit she would bring her kettle of coffee and her knitting. She knitted extraordinarily fast, faster than most other women. The more engrossed in her thoughts, the faster the needles worked their way through the wool. She did all her housework quickly, leaving time for her problems, which she sat and discussed with the ladies. She had a colourful way of speaking. Commenting on the neighbours whose husbands worked in Kuwait, she said, 'They leave these poor women alone all year and come once a year to inflate them and leave again.'

I was a weak, frail child, too small for my age. When we sat to eat lunch around the dining table, my father at the head, my mother next to him, I would refuse to eat. I suffered from diarrhoea and a bloated stomach. The feeling of being hollow and weak, with a vulnerable physique, was constant throughout my childhood. I envied those boys in my class who had strong, dependable bodies that made them feel robust and energetic.

When I started going to the Ahlia School around the corner

from our house, the big boys would follow me around, trying to open the clasp of my small box. My mother had given me a little wooden red box with a handle for my pencils, drawing book and sandwich. The boys kept coming and trying to open it and I would hold it away from them, but they were bigger and I could not stop them. Eventually one would succeed in opening it so that all the contents fell out. It embarrassed me to have things exhibited on the ground for all the other boys to see. One winter's day I couldn't wait to leave school and get home, so I set off without putting on my coat, even though it was raining. I dragged the wet garment behind me as I trudged back home. It was only a short distance to our house, so I didn't think it was necessary to wear the coat. I will soon be home, I thought, trailing it as it became heavy with rain. The house was further than I had thought. So I dropped my coat and arrived home dripping wet. My mother was livid with the teachers. How could they allow a four-year-old to leave without making sure that he had put on his coat? Next morning I was ill with pneumonia. My mother was so furious she never sent me back. A year later, when I was old enough, I was enrolled at the Friends School, a little further away.

After my bad experience at the Ahlia School I was given a leather bag to take with me. I was glad that the older boys had no curiosity about my bag, but I was still stuck with tiny feet that continued to be of interest to them. Boys would come over to check them out and measure them against their own. Yet none of this mattered, because I was more alive in my head than in the physical world around me.

During the summer holidays I stayed within the small world of our house and garden. I would look at the empty rolling hills to the front, which provided an unobstructed view to the horizon. I was fond of catching butterflies. As I ran after them I imagined myself running down the terraces all the way to Ayn

Musbah, the spring at which women lined up every morning to fill their jerrycans with water. The first story I wrote was about the adventures of a boy running after a butterfly, escaping the walled garden and going through thistles and down terraces into the wadi, then getting lost.

When I reached my early teens my father would stand me against the wall to measure my height. Our neighbour Dr Ghannam, with his ginger hair and freckled skin, made a mark on the wall where the top of my head came. Every few months he would check again, but the mark stayed in the same place. I could tell that my parents were concerned.

The late 1950s were the years of coffee-cup readings, when the women sat for hours over morning coffee, gossiping and knitting. When they finished drinking their Turkish coffee they turned the small cups over, letting the grounds slide down the sides, leaving intricate patterns from which my mother would read their fortunes and, in her lovely melodious voice, announce what was in store for them. After morning coffee the women would each go their separate ways. Then *Tata* could be heard calling from her house, wanting to know if we had tomatoes: 'I've run out of them. And could you also bring some mint leaves?'

When my father was banished from Jordan in 1955 because of his oppositional politics, we followed him to Beirut. There my weak health deteriorated further and it was thought best to send me back to Ramallah to live with *Tata*, while the rest of the family remained in Lebanon.

She cooked breakfast for me every day and made me eat it. 'You should get fat,' she would say in her imperious voice. She also brought in the nurse to give me a daily vitamin shot, so I called her Nadia Eiber (needle Nadia). I hated her and dreaded the injections. She swabbed my bottom with cotton wool and alcohol, stuck the needle in and kept it there. It hurt and so I cried. Then she pulled it out and said, 'See, it is all over.' And we would count how much longer before the next one and I would be comforted that there was still another day and night before the morning of the next day and the next shot. Nadia was rotund and spoke little. She left after she finished her task, taking with her the little bag with the dreaded needle and the medicine. She had a bad ending. When she retired, the doctor for whom she worked did not pay her the pension she was owed for her years of service. Impoverished, she died horribly after contracting gangrene and losing her leg.

With the family away, the house downstairs was quiet. I spent a lot of time alone with *Tata*, sleeping for long hours and taking naps after lunch. Now I lived upstairs, I was happy to be with my grandmother. She did not fuss over me but left me alone, except at mealtimes, when she made me eat. It was not possible to argue with her so I had no choice but to obey.

Whenever I hear the wind in the pines, I am reminded of the Grand Hotel. In the afternoons my grandmother and I would walk together to sit in the hotel's garden at the top of the hill from our house. It had old elegant buildings with a large pine tree garden in the back and a colourful front garden closer to the main building. We sat on green wicker chairs and my grandmother had tea which she flavoured with lemon verbena leaves that she asked me to pick for her from the nearby shrub as she chatted with Um Yousef, the proprietress, who stood by reverently watering the dahlias with a long hose. After she finished she paused, before calling with a cracked voice to the handyman, 'Rizq, Rizq, come turn off the water.' Then she came over and sat with my grandmother.

Um Yousef spoke with a Lebanese accent and was often unable to hold back her tears, which flowed down her cheeks. Even when she didn't cry her face remained sad. She couldn't stop thinking of the son she had lost and the older daughter who had had to be confined to a mental asylum. She had good reasons to be unhappy, yet she also grumbled about everything. My grandmother never cried or grumbled. She was content to be sitting in her wicker chair drinking tea with her yellow angora shawl wrapped around her shoulders. I would go off to play alone under the pines, finding things to look at and examine. 'He's no trouble, none at all,' my grandmother told Um Yousef. They spoke of Aida, her attractive younger daughter, with the glittering dark blue eyes, who was sprightly and always working, going from one part of the garden or the hotel to another in her colourful apron. Behind where they sat were the many hydrangea pots which were now concealed by curtains that the proprietress pulled back as soon as the afternoon sun began to wane.

Um Yousef, whom we always called Madame Audeh, was a proud Lebanese. When the women of the town came to offer their condolences for her son's death from cancer in the late 1950s, she threw them out. Yousef's death had been sudden, he was in the prime of life, and she could not be consoled. Everyone thought that she had lost her mind, the way she screamed and refused to receive people. 'Go back to where you came from,' she would yell at the top of her shrill voice. 'I don't want to see any of you here.' Madame Audeh never seemed to recover from the shock.

After the Israeli army withdrew from the hotel in 1968, a year after the beginning of the occupation, the hotel did not immediately reopen. Um Yousef would stand alone in the empty grounds as she tried to revive the garden and give way to her grief. She was thinking of her son and what he had planned for this place: a splendid hotel with a tennis court and nightclub. Even though a decade had passed since his death, she still couldn't stop grieving. The air of melancholy dominated the attractive grounds where the rose bushes were beginning to bud. Um Yousef held the hose as tears streamed down her cheeks. It took several years before the hotel reopened, but it never returned to its former glory. It was as though that brief stay by the Israeli army had robbed the place of the special aura and glamour that the old Lebanese woman and her determined daughter had worked so hard to cultivate.

When twilight fell and the light began to fade, Madame Audeh could be heard calling to Rizq to turn on the lights. She said this in a broken, despairing voice, as though she was weary of having to keep saying it every evening. The lights came on, a row of bulbs slung from tree to tree. But there were few lights in the back garden where the trees were denser and the sky was turning dark and forbidding. I returned from the garden and sat next to my grandmother. 'He is mine, mine,' she would announce to Madame Audeh, as she held me next to her, and I would lean over and rest my head on her angora shawl. The birds were twittering in the trees, getting ready to go to sleep. I was glad to discover that birds twitter before going to sleep. The tea had got cold and it was almost time for dinner. My grandmother said she had to go.

'No, Julia, stay a little longer.'

'They keep breaking the light on my street, these terrible boys, and I am afraid to slip and fall in the dark. I keep getting the municipality to fix it, but they throw stones and break it as soon as it gets fixed. I don't know what to do with these boys. So many bad boys in our street. They are not well brought up. Their mothers let them out in the street the whole day. I try to get my nap in the afternoon, but they scream at the tops of their voices. They allow me no rest. It is awful. I must leave now before it gets completely dark.'

And so we would walk home, down the street of Cinema Dunia to Main Street, past Ramallah's only florist.

On one occasion *Tata* noticed that Abu Iskandar was open and she walked towards him. 'Do you want a *shawarma*? I will buy you a *shawarma*.' What a treat, because I liked *shawarma*. Abu Iskandar always had a serious grin as he turned the skewer and examined the meat, then picked a good place and slid the sharpened knife down to slice the meat. 'Don't give him the fat, remove all the fat,' Tata instructed. Abu Iskandar did not look pleased about this. He took the spatula and scraped away the pieces of fat, pushing them to the side. He opened the long *hamam* (pigeon) bread and scooped up the fat-free meat. He added sliced onions spiced with sumac, then poked the sandwich with a fork and placed it by the fire to warm up. Finally, he pulled it out and wrapped it in paper before, with a turn of the hand, stooping down to give it to me. He seemed proud of his sandwich and serious about his work. My grandmother took one with the extra fat for herself and we ate our sandwiches in the street as we walked home, her cane tapping against the paving stones.

But that *shawarma* did not agree with me and I awoke with diarrhoea. Again I got that familiar feeling of weakness and hollowness, and I suffered from stomach cramps the whole day. My grandmother put me on a diet of potatoes and bread, while she ate a steak.

Tata spoke with a full voice and had a gap between her two front teeth. She liked to eat and had a strong constitution. Her balcony with its open view was refreshing and inviting. Sitting in her green wicker chair, she monitored the street, calling down to women she knew who were passing by and inviting them up. Then she would rush inside to brew Turkish coffee and bring it out on a round brown tray with two small cups, and the women would sip coffee and exchange news about the neighbours. One day the news was shocking.

Sophie, who lived up the hill, had gone to buy coffee from Zaibak's in the old city and found the shop closed. She asked his neighbour where he was and this neighbour jokingly answered, 'Gone to heaven.' So Sophie now had news to spread. She immediately went around telling everyone, 'Have you heard? Have you heard? Zaibak is dead.'

I remember Zaibak very well, a frail unassuming man standing in his shop, which was crowded with sacks of rice and sugar and other foodstuffs. He was often helped by his sister.

'Oh, really?' said the first woman Sophie met on the way. 'When did this happen?'

'Just this morning,' Sophie answered. 'I went down to buy coffee and found his shop closed. The neighbour told me the news. He said, "Zaibak died."'

'Poor man,' said the first woman, who began to walk more hurriedly so that she could get to the other women before Sophie and be the one to break the news.

My mother was the only one who was sceptical. 'Zaibak dead? Impossible,' she declared. 'It's not believable that a man like him would die so suddenly. He's not that sort of man.' And as confirmation of her position, she told the story of how one day she went to buy coffee from Zaibak and found another woman in his shop who wanted to buy rice. 'And you know what,' my mother said, 'Zaibak wouldn't sell her any.

'"But why won't you sell me rice?" the woman wanted to know.

'"Not today," Zaibak said in his offhand way. "Come back tomorrow."

'"But I need the rice this morning. I've run out of rice and I need it now."

'"I'm not selling you any rice this morning."

'"But why? Just tell me why?"

'"All day I have to put rice in a bag and weigh it, and if it's not rice then it's sugar. I don't feel like doing it now. Come back another time."

'"But I need some rice now," she insisted.

'"I don't care. I'm too bored doing the same thing all day."

'She kept insisting, but he adamantly refused to sell her the rice. Can such a man die?' my mother argued. 'Imagine, he gets tired and bored of selling rice and decides to go on strike and nothing will change his mind. This is a man who knows how to live. He's not the dying type.'

In the course of the morning Sophie had told so many people the 'news' that by the afternoon there was a large crowd at the Orthodox Church of Transfiguration, which had been built in 1850 in downtown Ramallah, close to Zaibak's shop. They were all dressed in black and wearing sombre faces to attend the funeral, but they found Zaibak standing there as usual, stooped behind the counter in his shop, his sister with the crooked teeth standing next to him. That morning he had gone round the corner to his house to use the toilet and had closed the door of his shop when Sophie happened to arrive, and the neighbour jokingly told her that Zaibak had gone to heaven.

Whenever my mother later repeated this story, she concluded it by saying, 'That day Zaibak died and rose from the dead just like Lazarus. And all because of Sophie's big mouth.'

From the late 1950s until the 1967 war, an Italian pop group performed at the Grand (as we affectionately began referring to the Grand Hotel) every Saturday and Sunday afternoon in the summer. They would break for a few hours and then resume in the evening. Now the sound of Quranic readings between the calls to prayer dominates the air most of the day. We would relax in the garden of the Grand, listening to the rustle of the pine trees and the twittering of birds. We had no doubt and felt strongly that the city was ours. After we went home the band would strike up at the hotel's open-air nightclub. I would fall asleep as they went on playing until late at night.

On weekdays in the Grand Hotel garden we could hear plenty of birds preparing to sleep high up in the pine trees as evening turned to night. Those were long, enchanted summer evenings when we lingered in the gorgeous surroundings. Sometimes father would decide to stay on for a glass of arak, which was served with a mezze of delicious small plates. Moving quietly between the tables at the Grand was a slight old man asking questions. For years the unassuming philan-thropist Aziz Shaheen did research for his book of genealogies. He would shuffle from table to table, pen and paper in hand, asking for information from the expats who had returned to Ramallah for a summer visit, about the names of new spouses, and the names and number of their children. When he finished he left. He never stayed around to enjoy the evening as the rest of us were doing. While very few of Ramallah's original people remain in the city, before Shaheen died he managed to complete and publish his book, which has preserved the names and lineages of the eight large families that established the city, most of whom are scattered in the diaspora. The town has developed into an anonymous city where a mix of residents and foreigners of different nationalities live. Shaheen died leaving an only son, Naseeb, who never married. He also died leaving no heirs. Aziz Shaheen will be remembered in Ramallah for his book, which has become the city's bible and his most-lasting legacy.

Among the many garden cafés in today's Ramallah, one of the most charming is owned by Amin Marouf, the son of the owner of the first flower shop, whose mother had lived in a most attrac-tive tent on Friends Street. It is situated in a pine garden on the outskirts of the city. Appropriately, it is called Snowbar, which in Arabic means pine. Yet despite the charm of sitting under a canopy of pines both here and in the Grand Hotel's garden, the newer place has less atmosphere than the Grand used to have. Perhaps that magic cannot be replicated, at least not with the wide projection screens showing bands playing incessant loud pop and rap music in Arabic and English. Frequently there are birthday celebrations accompanied by 'Happy Birthday' sung first in English and then in Arabic. Birthday celebrations used to be private affairs, mainly celebrated by the Christians in the privacy of their own home. Now they have become a public spectacle, adding to the noise and chaos in restaurants and cafés. Perhaps the noise is necessary to drown the fear and guilt at the neglect of public causes, like a drunk man wanting to forget all the surrounding misery. The stakes were never so high. Earlier, life was simpler. Perhaps, after fifty years of occupation, we now get drunk on loud noise.

The other night I was leaving another of Ramallah's famous restaurants, Darna, after a pleasant meal. There was a cool breeze and white cottony clouds in the sky. I started thinking that this has the makings of a very good city to live in, but there is no joy; pleasure is blunted by the sad events and incessant bad news that envelop us.

When one of my mother's favourite second-floor flats equipped with central heating in the centre of town became available we decided to rent it. After the occupation my mother felt safer living off the ground, because she still remembered the Jordanian police who came to arrest my father banging on the windows and insisting to be allowed in. She felt able to move away from the old house, leaving her mother alone in the upstairs flat, because she trusted that Sophie and her brother Harbi, who lived nearby, would keep an eye on her.

Sophie's family were three siblings who lived together, Sophie, Harbi and the eldest, Hanna. Their second-floor flat had a spacious terrace with three arches just up the hill from our old house. The elder brother had worked as a civil servant with the Mandate government. He was retired and was a recovering alcoholic. He observed a strict routine, was autocratic and demanded that his sister prepare three meals as well as afternoon tea, following which he would take a small stroll. So wherever Sophie happened to be visiting she had to rush back to feed him. He altered his routine only during the Israeli occupation, when he vowed that he would not leave his house until the Israelis withdrew.

For years he would sit on the balcony with the arches overlooking a garden planted with pine trees and a floor of white-and-black-chequered tiles. Several years into the 1967 occupation, my mother happened to meet him on the street.

'How come you're out of the house?' she asked. 'Have the Israeli soldiers left?'

'Oh, no,' he said. 'It's just that I have a dental appointment.' Then he proudly boasted to my mother, 'Do you see this suit?'

My mother said yes.

'Well, would you believe I've had it for twenty years? And yet see how it still looks like new.'

'But of course it would,' said my mother. 'It's been hanging in the wardrobe unused for the past ten years.'

Hanna did not care for the Arabic soap operas on television and would not allow his siblings to watch them. That was why they escaped to *Tata*'s house every night to watch whichever ones they were following. Harbi, the younger brother, had also worked with the Mandate civil service. He was at the headquarters in the King David Hotel in Jerusalem when it was blown up by Jewish terrorists. With his soft humming voice and unassuming manner, he described his experience as he sat in the green wicker chair with his sister and my grandmother: 'I heard the huge explosion. The room I was working in filled with dust and when I could see I realised the floor had broken in half. The half where my desk was remained in place. Beyond it everything had collapsed. I stood there on the edge in shock, breathing dust.'

He was a lucky man. In that bombing ninety-one people were killed, of whom twenty-one were senior government officials, thirteen were soldiers, three policemen and fifty-four members of the public: typists, clerks, messengers, employees of the hotel and canteen workers. Of the total killed, forty-one were Palestinian. Harbi was spared.

My grandmother had strong opinions about everything. She never grumbled, ate well, took a nap after lunch and went out visiting every afternoon. If she had no one to visit she went to the Grand Hotel, where she had tea for five piastres, with another piastre for a tip. She always had flowers in her crimson-coloured glass vase at home. She loved flowers and was a good gardener.

Unlike my mother, she was confident and not at all anxious. She often reprimanded others but she didn't complain. My mother was different, unhappy about many things, but primarily my father. We would be waiting for lunch and my mother would be tired and bored. 'He doesn't like to come home,' she would say. 'He delays on purpose to annoy me. I have everything ready for him and he doesn't come. He says he's coming but doesn't. I have to keep reheating the food again and again. I am so tired of him and his ways. You should not grow up to be like your father,' she would tell me. 'Why does he not like coming home? He hates coming home, hates his home. I do everything to make it pleasant for him but he runs away. He likes the office. He wants to be in the office the whole time. He makes me so tired.' I would listen and sympathise with my mother and promise to grow up to be a better man.

One day we heard my grandmother screaming, 'Go away, you dirty old man.' We went up to check. It was Abu Nabil, the guard at the bus park on the hill. 'He came into my house and touched himself. What does he take me for? Dirty old man. I threw him out and told him never to set foot in this house. He hurtled down the stairs limping, the dirty old man. Look at me,' she said, 'I am shaking, shaking with rage.'

He was not the only visitor she scolded. There was another episode with the newspaper man, Abu Al Habayeb, with his *serwal* and his dirty old grey-green jacket, who always carried the newspapers under his arm. He climbed *Tata* Julia's stairs and saw that she was in the kitchen. He told her to open the window so he could lean over and hand her the newspaper. When he stretched his body to reach out, his garment split at the seams and my grandmother could see that he did not have any underwear on. 'What is this, you dirty old man?' she called out. 'You must never come back here. You hear me, never come back. You have no shame. No shame.' Reading the daily paper had to be sacrificed. No! My grandmother was not a mere villager from Ramallah. Heaven forbid. She was from the city of Haifa, the daughter of a hotelier. Heaven help whoever dared say she was from Ramallah.

Living next to the Harbs' house was a man from Jaffa who owned a Buick. There were so few cars in our city then that it was possible to count all of them and know who a car belonged to when it passed. Car owners were a class unto themselves, known to everyone. People were identified by their cars: 'He's the one who owns the Ford' or 'He drives the VW *sarsour*' (cockroach). There was only one Buick, a sky-blue 1948 model, and its owner was our neighbour. He bought the car just before the Nakba, when he could afford it. After the disaster and his impoverishment, he could not find a buyer and so for a short time, when the road to Jaffa was still open, he used it as a taxi to ferry people and make some money. When the road to Jaffa closed he decided that he would not use it again until the roads reopened. That car remained parked, never to be used. It was kept in a garage he rented from my grandmother.

One morning this neighbour with the revered old blue Buick climbed up the stairs to my grandmother's house. From her kitchen window, Julia saw that his cheeks were smudged with tears. He looked terribly distraught, panting as he climbed the stairs and calling, 'Um Emile, Um Emile.'

'What is it?' Julia asked, rushing to open the door, concerned that some great calamity had befallen her neighbour.

'*Ya*, Um Emile,' he started in a plaintive tone.

'What is it? What's wrong? Tell me, has anything happened to your wife?'

'*Ya*, Um Emile,' he began again, 'you are well aware of the economic situation. I am suffering like everyone else. I implore you, can you reduce the rent?'

'What rent?' asked my grandmother.

'The garage rent,' he answered.

'What!' screamed Julia in his face. 'You come all this way, climb all these stairs, to ask for a reduction in a rent of one dinar? All you're paying is one dinar and you want me to reduce this? Are you out of your mind? You should be ashamed of yourself, an old man like you, coming all this way to plead for a reduction in a rent of one dinar.' And she sent him scurrying off down the stairs, showering him with words intended to shame him into never repeating his request.

I will always remember fondly these episodes that were repeated so often in the intimate friendly neighbourhood where I grew up. For many years I persisted in idealising life there, where everyone knew everyone else and took great pleasure in the bickering, the long morning-coffee visits and the gossip, believing that it was the sort of life I had envisaged living in my city. But it wasn't. It was not at all what I wanted.

I was never someone who fulfilled his social duties towards the community, who went to funerals and weddings, or who knew how to make small talk. I stayed away from social gatherings. I did not open my house to many visitors, a practice expected and appreciated by my society. Penny and I have lived a largely private life, which we both absolutely needed in order to carry on with our writing.

Standing outside our old house, where I spent the crucial years of my life, more memories came flooding back. The old metal garden gate was unchanged after all these years. The houses up the hill where the Harbs and the owner of the Buick had lived were still standing. But the sky-blue car was not there. I stood beneath the pines, enjoying the all too familiar sound of the soft breeze blowing through their branches, and I thought I could hear opera coming out of the closed windows and my mother's voice asking my father to lower the volume. How strange this music must have sounded to the other people around us. And I remembered my sisters with their red velvet dresses and white collars, and my parents, both well dressed, going to their black Mercedes for an evening out.

I was glad to have come to this breezy part of town and lingered, absorbing the atmosphere. What a romantic I had been, incomplete in myself and captured by that enchanted world to which for many years I remained hostage. Among other things, that world had appeared to offer sociability that served as a shield against being alone. For as long as possible I tried to delay getting out of it. When I finally did leave I thought that I had lost and became unfeeling. It has taken me a long time to accept my solitude. Yeats described poetry as a social act of the solitary man. In time I came to realise that my writing served that same purpose.

This neighbourhood is one of the few in Ramallah that has remained more or less as I remembered it. I could imagine myself as a little boy, feeling the refreshing wind, breathing the clean Ramallah air and thinking that all this would last forever. Time went by so much more slowly then. Is this why one yearns, as one gets older, to return to old haunts, to re-experience that sense of slow time?

The present inhabitants of our old house have the most messy garden. It is cluttered with all sorts of abandoned objects without a single plant in sight. Behind the old stone wall there are broken tables, chairs, pipes, plastic containers full of holes, rusty wire, cardboard, pieces of wood, trunks and branches of trees, bicycle wheels and an old stained toilet seat.

In my mind's eye I clear out the rubbish and see a happy sight: my father wearing dark brown trousers and a white shirt and my mother wearing a red-and-white striped jumper, standing apart in the garden beneath the Syrian pines. Between them is my fourteen-month-old brother, with his curls and red cheeks bursting with health. He is taking his first steps between them. Their arms are wide open, ready to receive him, and their faces glow with pride. They show more happiness than I can ever remember them exhibiting and all thanks to my brother, for it was he, not I, who was the more gratifying son, the one closer to my father, the apple of his eye. Nearby is the patch of cress that I had planted from seed in my enduring attempts to win favour with my father, because he had said he enjoyed eating it.

Then another memory follows from the early 1980s, when I was in my thirties – long after I had left the magical world of my childhood, but before I had succeeded in finding my authentic self. It is of my grandmother, who had shown such kindness to me when I was young, being carried away on a stretcher to a waiting ambulance. The orderlies who were bringing her down the stairs were being rough. Every movement hurt. My strong grandmother, who never cried, shouted to them to be more careful. The orderlies were indifferent. She moaned from the excruciating pain she was suffering. My sister Samar, who was standing next to me, said mournfully, with a lot of pain in her voice, '*Tata* will never be returning to her house.' And I, the disappointed romantic, stood there stiff and numb, unable to grieve. How could I have been so insensitive and callous towards the woman I loved?

Seven

I needed an espresso. I walked uphill from our old house, turned right on to Ahlia Street, named after the Ahlia School which I attended for a few weeks as a child, and climbed to the fifth floor of the building opposite the old school gate to Capers Restaurant, owned by Ramzi and Nahida Jaber's sons. On the terrace an olive tree was planted in a large pot that could be rolled in and out for the summer and winter seating. From there I had a panoramic view of this part of Ramallah, of our old *hara* and beyond to the Mediterranean coast, with Tel Aviv's high-rises lining the horizon. At one time it was possible to enjoy this view from the ground. Not any more. Now the ground has to be suggested by placing an olive tree in a large pot on the fifth floor; only then can one see it.

Ramzi Jaber was a rich, down-to-earth romantic. He loved birds and kept a thriving aviary until fear of bird flu made him dispose of all of them to protect his family. It was a sad day for him but he felt he owed it to his children and grandchildren. Before he died he tried to purchase all the empty plots and houses in his *hara* to preserve it as he knew it. His success was only partial. He purchased the house where the Harbs used to live, with its long front balcony. Had he not bought it, it would certainly have been sold to others and repurposed. The previous owners, the Totah family, had emigrated to the US, all except two of the sons. Their father was a brilliant electrician who was renowned for working extremely fast. After my father helped him with a legal dispute and refused to charge him, we returned home one afternoon to find that he had replaced all our electric switches with new fluorescent ones. Next to the Harbs' house, the one where the Bahu family lived was still standing. The father had owned the sky-blue Buick. For years after his death it remained parked in the driveway. Only one of the sons has remained in Ramallah; the others are in the US. Even Najla Al Bansa is no longer there. The building I was now in had been erected on the land where her shack once stood.

The only house Ramzi could not buy was the one across the street from our old house, where we moved two years prior to the start of the occupation. It was there that my father drafted the first proposal for a Palestinian state to be established in the 1967 occupied territories and submitted it to the Israeli government. The house where this historic event took place was demolished soon after the Oslo Accords came into force. A telling coincidence.

Many people from Ramallah who emigrated to the US return only to sell their land. And when they sell, they do little to contribute to the city's development. They do not pay capital gains or capital transfer taxes to the Palestinian Authority. And many manage to find ways to smuggle out the money so that they don't have to report the proceeds of the sale for US taxes either.

I asked for the bill and paid the equivalent of a Jordanian dinar (£1.10) for my coffee. When I was growing up a dinar meant a lot to us. Despite the fact that my family had to deal with difficult conditions after the Nakba, they kept their pride and dignity. I was never made to feel inferior to anyone or felt I had to look up to those who were materially better off. Surely my parents' life would have been happier had they not been forced out of Jaffa. The combination of personal tragedies and economic straits that left my grandmother in the care of my mother and forced us to live in cramped lodgings made for trying conditions.

At one point my parents were so short of cash that my mother had to sell one of her rings. The only goldsmith in Ramallah at the time was Abu Jirius, whose workshop was in a stone building on Main Street. You climbed two high steps to enter. The workshop was in the back, the display area, where the gold was sold, in front. The tight-fisted old man still wore a *serwal*. My mother always said she did not get a fair price for her diamond ring, which she had brought with her from Jaffa. She was loath to part with it, yet at the time she had no option. Stories about this man's avarice and meanness proliferated. One day a friend of his from a nearby village came to visit. It was after the Nakba, when the economic situation was bad for most people. When the friend entered his shop, they embraced and the man said, 'I have a favour to ask of you.'

Abu Jirius replied, 'Ask whatever you want.'

'You know how bad the situation is. I need to borrow 100 dinars from you.'

'Why not?'

And he counted the money out and put the pile of notes on the counter.

The man was thrilled. But when he reached for the money, Abu Jirius put down his hand over it. 'No,' he said.

'Why?' asked the man. 'What's the matter?'

'Not before you kiss my hand. You cannot take the money until you've kissed my hand.'

'Why?' asked the man. 'Why are you asking me to kiss your hand?'

'Because before I get it back I'll have to kiss your arse, so I want to get this kiss now before it's too late.'

After paying for the espresso I took the lift down to the street, intending to head off to Main Street and retrace the steps I used to take as a child with my grandmother when we returned from an afternoon at the Grand Hotel.

Ahlia Street was congested with Mercedes and BMWs that were most likely financed by loans from the Cairo Amman Bank, whose branch was in the lower floor of the building I had just left. Negotiating his way between these fancy cars was a bent old man. He didn't appear to know what he was doing and seemed to be circling around the slowly moving line of traffic as though he was lost. He was overweight and he hobbled. His red cheeks were puffed and he had a vacant look in his eyes. He had a lot of ginger hair on his head that could have been dyed with henna. He seemed bewildered. Then I noticed someone going to rescue him from the maze of vehicles. The old man looked familiar. I caught up with him and, looking more closely, realised it was Abu Hassan, whose family were renting the house we once lived in. He had a frozen grin, with eyes focused on his next conquest. A pair of open scissors dangled from his belt. I didn't feel like greeting him, for fear of getting caught in endless chatter, and instead decided to retrace my steps to Ahlia Street and follow him to see whether he still lived in our old house.

At the corner just before starting downhill, Abu Hassan stopped. He stooped down and picked up an empty plastic water bottle that was lying by the pavement. I admired his public spirit in picking up rubbish. He ambled over towards the green recycling bin, deposited the bottle carefully beside it, then tried to poke about inside. But it was too high for him, so he held on to the sides and made to pull himself up. He couldn't manage that, so he stood on tiptoe, sliding up and down and losing his balance. What was he doing? He was clearly not going to throw away the rubbish he had picked up in the street. Then I saw him extend his right hand and rummage through things. He pulled up an old wooden chair, but it was too heavy to retrieve with one hand so he dropped it. Then he went away and returned with a rock. He stood on it, bent down and scooped out the chair with both hands, pulled it up and dropped it on the ground next to the plastic bottle. This seemed to exhaust him. He stepped down from the rock and took a breath. Then he looked for the bottle and slipped it under his arm. Clutching the chair, which I now saw was half burnt, he set off, dragging it behind him.

When he reached the corner, the neighbours' boys saw him approaching, left the garden where they were playing and came running. 'Abu Hassan, Abu Hassan, here is an iron rod we found for you,' one of them said.

He turned to look. As he began to examine it, another boy came up with a cardboard box. 'For you, Abu Hassan, for you.'

Soon there was a throng of boys, like an army of rubbish collectors, each with something for the old man, who stood among them like the commander of trash. They were laughing and enjoying themselves. Abu Hassan was befuddled. As each of the boys approached, he examined carefully the booty, reluctant to waste any of these offerings, though he must have known that they were making fun of him. Abu Hassan led the procession, still with his prized possessions, the burnt wooden chair he dragged behind him and the bottle under his arm, and the boys followed closely, carrying the rest. I followed too, though I kept at a safe distance. Once the old man was behind the gate of his house, the one we had lived in, the boys dramatically threw their items over the wall in turn, crying, 'Here, Abu Hassan, take, enjoy.'

I was worried that something would hit him, burying him beneath a pile of trash, but the boys were not malicious. Now that the man had gone, the party was over. They turned and ran back up the hill into their garden. I lingered. I could not imagine what use any of these items could be to Abu Hassan's family. But it seemed that, out of habit, this hoarder dragged something back with him every time he went home. The yard was already so full of junk, if the old man lived much longer it would spill over into the house.

Hoarding has now been classified as a medical disorder, characterised by an 'accumulation of possessions due to excessive acquisition of or difficulty discarding possessions regardless of their actual value'. Abu Hassan was most definitely afflicted. In retrospect, I should have been more sympathetic, especially because I too have that tendency.

Returning to Main Street, I stopped at the corner by the Karameh sweet shop and café. My office was just a five-minute walk from here, but it was still too early for my meeting. I lingered and scanned the row of shops close to the office, some of which have been there since I was a child. I could see Hinn's barber shop with Iskandar, whom I have known since he was a boy studying at the Ahlia School, sitting on a chair outside his shop, sunning himself. This was an opportunity to have a haircut without having to wait my turn. I crossed the street and walked over.

He had started working with his father just after finishing his studies at university. Now he worked with his two younger brothers. A few years ago his father collapsed and died at work after a massive heart attack. Iskandar had tried to save him but failed. I remember how he described to me washing his father's corpse before the burial. This was his last service to his father, with whom he had worked side by side for many years. To wash the body prior to sending his father to the grave was an opportunity for a real farewell before going ahead with his own life. I listened to him saying all this, aware that I had failed to give a similar parting to my own father. Perhaps, had I done so, I wouldn't spend so much time looking backwards.

As I sat on the traditional heavy barber's chair, I could see how many more of my hairs were white as they fell on the black robe in which I was wrapped. When I looked up, my eye caught sight of the photograph of Iskandar's father on the wall. It's traditional to hang a picture of the deceased in his last place of work. One can see pictures of dead fathers in the hardware shop, the sandwich place and at the fruit juicer's. When my father died, I broke with tradition and did not put up his picture on the wall, even though I continued to work in the same office. I felt his strong presence throughout the office; it could not be confined to a single picture hanging on the wall. After I moved from my small room to my father's more spacious one with the large old wooden desk, friends of his visiting from abroad who stopped by, hoping to see him, commented on the close physical resemblance between us: 'You are the spitting image of your father. If only you would gain more weight you would be like a carbon copy.' They stared as though looking through me at him, even when I had done away with the dark curtains that created a dim background and replaced them with more cheerful hangings on the wall. Nowadays I can see more of this resemblance when I look in the mirror. My grin and the grooves around my mouth are giving me that same forlorn look that my father's face began to have at around the age I am now. How sad that times have not improved, confirming all our worst fears. Perhaps in view of the close resemblance between us, I could be forgiven for failing to hang my father's picture on the wall above my desk.

In the chair to my left, Issa, Iskandar's younger brother, was attending to a sixteen-year-old who was getting his first shave. I was reminded how shy I was when the man in the picture on the wall asked me whether I wanted my moustache shaved. This boy was not at all embarrassed. He was proud of his facial hair and was boasting about how he managed to mobilise his cousins for an attack against boys who sent threats to his Facebook page. Issa listened in silence without commenting. But the paternal Iskandar turned to the young man and said, in a preaching voice, 'Just remember that it is only the weak who do not forgive.' There was a pause, then Iskandar followed this with more advice, saying that in future he would do well to show such messages to his parents.

'My father is always against me. Only once did he side with me,' the young man said.

'Why didn't you tell your teachers or the headmaster about this?'

The young man answered, 'I would have been dismissed for bringing *shabab* [young men] from outside the school on to the school grounds.'

I looked more carefully at the father's picture on the wall. I could see a strong resemblance with Issa, the less talkative brother, who throughout the exchange continued to perform his work in silence.

When I was done with the haircut I turned right, walking towards the old city. Soon I got to the corner of Friends Street, which leads to my old school. But I didn't want to go that way. Instead I continued straight along Main Street, passing by a Chinese restaurant on the corner run by young proprietors who had worked in Israel at a similar establishment. They were mixing sliced vegetables and slivers of meat in a wok to make a stir-fry. It was there that Batshoun's upmarket textile shop had been, where my mother used to go to buy material for her dresses.

I can still see her marching down Main Street with a strong sense of mission, her stiff rectangular handbag dangling from her left arm, which she held up against her waist as though its sole purpose was to serve as a hanger for that gleaming black bag.

I also remember how bright-faced Batshoun would meet her with a broad artificial smile, his round puffed cheeks glowing with health. At that time most people bought fabric and had their clothes made by tailors who were scattered all over the town, their number in proportion to the town's population. Few of these places had mannequins in their shop windows, but Batshoun did. Women could be more imaginative with their clothing. How many trips my mother would take to this and other shops before she made up her mind which fabric to buy. Half the stock would be unfurled and spread over the counter as she disdainfully lifted one piece after another with her long fingers while the owner looked on expectantly, wondering whether or not he was going to make a sale today. I could tell that in her mind's eye she was trying to imagine herself in the dress that she had conceived for herself. Eventually, when she had narrowed down the choice, she would pick up the whole roll and ask Batshoun to carry it for her to the long mirror where she stood. Then she would spread the cloth over her body, put one leg in front of the other, arch up her right foot and pose. In the mirror I could see my mother making a sweet face and the head of the owner behind her, with a big grin, exclaiming how well these colours suited her complexion and the tones of her hair, waving his fingers gracefully through the air near her face to emphasise the point: 'Madame Shehadeh, these colours are perfect. They suit you. And this fabric is the best. It was made especially for you.' There would be a tense moment as my mother paused before she thrust the material away, rejecting it, only to have the whole process begin once again at the next stop down the road.

In Jaffa my mother had Dora, a Jewish seamstress. In Ramallah she had Um Azmi, a real artist in dressmaking who made the most beautiful dresses. She lived off Irsal (broadcasting) Street in the northeastern part of Ramallah. The house was surrounded by a cluster of pine trees. She had a very old and tranquil husband who had a pharmacy in Main Street that must not have been doing well because his was one of the few shops left without a plastic awning when all the other shops installed them. A few years earlier, the couple had lost a son. The dressmaker once told my mother that the only way she could forget that moment, when he was brought dead to the house on a stretcher, was to work all the time. She had the saddest, most intense face of a woman I ever knew, but she was an artist in her own right, as her daughter, Samia, also turned out to be.

Years later, when I looked at the old family photographs, I couldn't help thinking how odd it was that in this small town of Ramallah there were people like my parents who dressed so fancily and hosted such dancing parties. My mother had a red and black pleated dress which was fit to wear at a real ball. My sisters had those red velvet dresses with stiff white collars, while I wore the golf trousers that made me look hilarious. And all this at a time when the place was impoverished and my parents were not so well off. Now that I've experienced my share of difficult times, I cannot but admire how, in a small town with limited resources, they lived it up, hosted parties, dressing well and managing, despite everything, to have a good time.

Somehow my parents found ways to keep themselves entertained and for my mother to show off her carefully tailored dresses. She would put on a dress in the evening and father would be wearing a suit, then they would go out for the night. We, the children, would be left alone in the house, having been told to 'lock up well'.

My eldest sister would be responsible for us. I slept top to tail in the same bed with my younger sister and our older sister slept alone in the bed next to us. One night, we heard movement in the house and someone walking up the stairs to my grandmother's house. My elder sister left her bed and went to call my parents. She was brave. I cowered in bed, half asleep. In the morning they said they could see footprints on the stairs. It was a thief, they said. A thief coming to burgle us at night.

Where do thieves stay, I wondered, when they're not stealing from others? Once we were visiting a place on the edge of town and someone pointed out across the valley and said all the thieves lived there. I wanted them to stay there always and never return to our house. But I was always afraid when I was alone at home with my sisters.

My father didn't like to stay at home in the evening. He worked hard and when his work was over he liked to go out. 'Where shall we go tonight?' he would ask my mother as soon as he came back from the office. He felt too confined and bored in the crowded house. When they didn't go out they entertained friends at home. Then everyone got busy and the small trays of food kept on coming and being taken away and others brought in. My father played loud music, often opera, and the whole house would be full of laughter and noise, though my mother remained anxious. In the mornings the house was stuffy with the lingering stench of tobacco smoke and the embers from the previous night's open fire.

Further down the street I passed by Al Haq's headquarters, which have now expanded to occupy offices on both sides of the street. I saw the impressive large sign: 'Al Haq, Palestinian affiliate of the International Commission of Jurists, Geneva'. As I looked at the sign, part of me felt proud that I had been instrumental in establishing this organisation. At the outset our

work conditions were difficult in ways that those now running
Al Haq can hardly imagine. Sending reports without a functioning postal service, fax or internet was an ordeal. Manu-
scripts had to be smuggled out, presenting great danger if they
were discovered at the border points. Even getting a telephone
line was problematic. And yet we pressed on. Sometimes I
wonder whether all the massive amount of documentation and
legal analysis the organisation completed over the years was of
any real consequence. After fifty years the occupation has not
ended and indeed has only become more entrenched. Still, it
can be said that, through its work, Al Haq has guaranteed that
Israel's illegal practices have not gone unnoticed or undocu-
mented. Reading what we have published will remove any
mystery as to how Israel succeeded in bringing about the legal
changes that now prevail. Information about Israeli practices
is recorded in thousands of affidavits, copies of which have
been sent to a safe archive abroad, so they cannot be seized
by soldiers and destroyed. Part of me is proud to have been
part of that struggle, but I remain sceptical that we might have
deceived ourselves into thinking human rights activism had real
promise, because the violations have only continued and indeed
increased. In terms of stopping more human rights violations,
our struggle has ended as a futile endeavour. All my work in
human rights could not deter that soldier from killing seventeen-year-old Nadeem Nowara. So sure was his killer that he
would not be prosecuted that he did not hesitate to publicly
declare that he had killed this young man out of boredom. Nor
did it deter the settlers from taking more Palestinian land and
using it for agriculture, employing the very people they took it
from, abandoning the oft-repeated fiction that Israel was taking
Palestinian lands for security reasons.

   Al Haq is now preparing the case for presentation to the
International Criminal Court against Israel for war crimes. If

there can be success in one case this would make a huge difference and would surely deter more soldiers from so brazenly
violating Palestinian human rights.

As I walk down the road I can see that the metal covers of the
manholes in the pavement have Arabic writing on them. A
decade ago Ramallah finally got a sewage system and this has
practically rid the city of annoying mosquitoes. In the past by
law every house had to have a cistern to collect rainwater and
a cesspit: two holes in the ground. The first was shaped like a
pear. The second was a hole in the ground with an unsealed
bottom, designed to enable water to drain from the sewage
and then escape into the ground, leaving the solids to dry and
disintegrate in a catchment area near the top. Depending on the
size of the hole, every so often a sewage truck would come and
pump out the smelly stuff.

Prior to the occupation we had no mosquitoes. I often
made the seemingly exaggerated claim that mosquitoes came
to our city with the Israeli soldiers. Yet it is true. Before the
war we would be sitting around in our *saha* (yard) when the
small, narrow-shouldered, bespectacled man we called 'the
kerosene man' would come swinging a small kerosene can he
was carrying and proceed immediately, with a strong sense of
mission, to our cesspit. Without uttering a word, he would
solemnly lift up the lid and pour kerosene inside. The kerosene
would float over the sewage and prevent mosquitoes from
breeding. The disruption in municipal activities brought about
by the war and the occupation meant that the little man with
the kerosene can stopped coming and the mosquitoes proliferated, just like the number of Israeli soldiers in our midst,
and for many decades this changed how we felt about the cool
summer evenings and the possibility of sitting outside without
being bitten. Now, with a better-functioning municipal council,

Ramallah is a more well-organised and livable place, with many garden restaurants where one can enjoy the good weather without being bothered by mosquitoes ... or soldiers.

I carry on down the street. This part has remained more or less the same as it was when I was a child. On the right-hand side, going up to the centre of town, is the building owned by Ramzi Jaber. Here there is a spice shop managed by Saleh Khalaf and another building owned by the Order of St Joseph, both of which are as they were in the 1950s. When I reach Khalaf's shop, which has been handed down from generation to generation, I am overwhelmed by the smell from the grinding of *zaatar* (thyme). Saleh inherited the shop from his father and has kept it exactly as it was, with the old herb grinders, sacks of different kinds of seeds by and outside the door on the pavement, and inside small drawers where he keeps different spices that are not marked but he knows immediately where each is. I stop to greet the owner and congratulate him on the many shops selling herbs that his sons have opened in other parts of town. They are among the few who went to the US and managed to return and start businesses in Ramallah. 'My sons,' he tells me, 'have the bodies of Palestinians and the minds of Americans. That's why they're successful.'

Most pedestrians scurry along as if they are being pursued. Except, that is, for old Karam of the button shop, who in 1948 was forced from Jaffa, where he also owned a haberdashery shop. He passes me on the way to his shop. His back is now completely bent and he uses a cane. Out of long habit, he is still one of the first to get to his shop, open it and then sit there all day, his drooping head leaning out of the door, almost falling into his lap. The whole day might pass without any customers entering to disturb his doze. I feel certain that he is a candidate for the next picture on the wall of another of Ramallah's shops. Except for him, though, everyone is walking as if possessed. In the past people would dawdle, stop and chat, linger and enjoy their time on the street. The way the shop owners used to behave, the way they used to drive in the 1950s and early 1960s, conveyed a sense of belonging, a feeling that the city was theirs.

I too used to charge briskly from my law office down to Al Haq, just along the street. I used to be full of energy and hope. I would look at the older people in town and think, I never want to be like that – sombre, bent, sad, defeated. I always wanted to look buoyant, smiling, surging through the streets to carry on with my next task, feeling a sense of great purpose that distinguished me.

Much as I want to believe it, it's not true that I walk invisible in the streets of Ramallah. I'm constantly being watched and observed by others. All eyes in such a small city are on everyone else, and this includes me. I have been walking these same streets all my life. The shop owners who see me passing by have all figured out how old I am. For many years they have been watching my progress, my process of ageing, my well-being, my health and how I'm keeping, as well as my pretensions and disguises, especially my hats. To others I might seem unable to decide who I am and how I want to appear, whether young, flamboyant, sombre, rich, neat, writerly or distinguished. Men my age here never appear in public except in suits. Jamil, my biology teacher at school, who, like me, was short and frail, and his brother the lawyer, who was also small, never appeared without a dark suit with a long jacket to give them stature. But what others see is only the outside appearance. These days, my inside and outside are not in sync. Inside I think of my face as bright and relaxed, even funny; from the outside it appears serious and rather sad, not funny at all. I used to have a smirk on my face, a triumphant look. Then it dissipated and I was left with a forlorn countenance. This is my face now.

The other day I went out to run some errands and I saw a

man who used to work in a grocer's where I shopped. He was walking very slowly, holding a cane. He had sunken cheeks and looked like one of the walking dead. Slowly, without moving his head, he turned and, with milky eyes, looked at me as if to remind me that now it's him but some day it will be me.

Another day I stopped by the Golden Thimble and left some clothes for mending. The energetic young son was not there. The no less energetic father took them and I gave him my name in case he didn't know it. After I left I asked myself, if he forgets my name, how would he describe me to his son? Probably as 'that older man, short, the one who wears funny hats'. Nothing about what I do is known to most of the people I meet on the street or with whom I do business in the shops nearby. Better that way.

But for now I can say that I've never felt better. Now that I'm on a gluten-free diet, I feel so much healthier. It has worked wonders. To think how long I've suffered in ignorance, blaming nuts for the bloating in my stomach. But the ravages of age are beginning to become evident, in the weakening eyesight, the veins and who knows what else.

As I ponder these thoughts I meet a former classmate of mine. He looks like an old man, with large jowls, some front teeth missing and eyes that lacked brightness.

'How is your health?' I ask.

'As long as I can walk and breathe, I thank God, and consider that I'm all right.'

'That is all you hope for?'

'That is all,' he says.

Then he complains about the high price of everything and tells me that his son had been working in Saudi Arabia but is back now. For a year and a half he's been sitting at home without work. 'He needs to work to find a wife. Who'll want to marry an unemployed man?'

I ask him about his brother Nabeel. He says he's been in the US since 1976. 'Why would he want to come back? What's there to come back for? What's good in this country?'

'What about the weather?' I say.

'What about the high price of everything?' he retorts.

Then he begins to complain about the internal migration, which he says is destroying the city.

'Can you blame them for wanting to leave Jenin after what happened there?' I ask.

'The civil servants take a supplement over their salary for living in Ramallah because they're supposed to be living in Jenin. They use it to take out a mortgage to buy a flat here. On Thursday they go back to Jenin and return on Sunday, having done all their shopping there where it's cheaper. What does the city get? Nothing. Look at the child's dress in this window. Here it's sold for fifty shekels. In Jenin it'll be twenty and that's because the shop owner in Ramallah has to pay much higher prices for everything.'

I leave my former classmate, who seems to have become a grumpy old man, and continue walking down a narrow street where there are some old craft shops. I turn left on Issa Ziadeh Street, named after the mayor of the late 1990s, who was also my brother's father-in-law. At the corner I pass what is called the Ottoman Courthouse, a renovated Ottoman building dating from the mid-nineteenth century. It was first used as a clinic, then as a *khan* (a building that functioned during Ottoman times as a trading centre and hostel, with stabling provided) and finally as a court of law headed by the regional director, Ahmad Murad Haken, appointed by the Ottoman government, with the lower floors serving as stables. Before its renovation in 2002, a single horse used to be kept in a dim, humid room on the ground floor. Penny and I would stop and greet it.

I walk on, passing the lower gate of the Friends School

and then an attractive pub called Berlin, which occupies an old building. Opposite the pub is a large sign that's lit up at night and proudly asserts the inclusive nature of the city. It is written in red letters with a white 'R': We Ramallah. No one stops to ask why a sign for a Palestinian city should be written in English rather than Arabic. But then people seem to like it, judging from the large numbers who come here to have their photos taken. Certainly Ramallah has become welcoming of different sorts of people, who arrive from all over Palestine and abroad and feel accepted.

I stop at the crossroads. The Roman Catholic church is on my right, at the corner of Kamal Adwan Street, named after one of three PLO members who were murdered by the Mossad on 10 April 1973, Adwan in his flat in Beirut, in front of his wife. Ahead is the Ramallah municipality's recently expanded building, now dubbed City Hall. On the lovely open terrace overlooking the small but attractive Ramallah municipal park, I stop by the stiff and ugly compact statue of Rashid Haddadeen, the purported founder of the city, with his wife next to him and six children representing Ramallah's founding family.

The jacarandas are plentiful in the southern part of the city and I want to have a look before their blooms vanish. But now I have to rush because I don't have much time left before my meeting. I cross the long Jaffa Road, which begins at Yasser Arafat Square in the centre of town. In the late 1930s the road connecting Ramallah to Jaffa was completed. It now leads to nearby Beitunia, beyond which the road is blocked by the Ofer checkpoint where Nadeem Nowara was shot dead.

Near the top of the road, I stop at the house of the late Aziz Shaheen, a true philanthropist who lived thriftily, walking everywhere, never taking a taxi, in order to save money, all of which he gave away to worthy causes and institutions. He was a kind, frail, unassuming man, single-minded with a will of iron.

118

Such a man, I thought, deserves the longest street in his name. But these are reserved for those who took part in the nationalist struggle. The municipality, instead, named a roundabout after him.

I continue southward behind Jaffa Road and sure enough the streets there are lined with the flowering purple trees. I decide to wander around a little enjoying the blooms before turning back.

Eight

In that low-lying section of Ramallah that was once a cultivated valley, behind Aziz Shaheen's home, there are still some of the old houses with their gardens. One of them belongs to two American friends, Susan Rockwell and Sharry Lapp, who have been living here for the past twenty years while volunteering their services for various projects in Palestine. They are both dedicated gardeners. Their single-floor house is surrounded by a large garden which I have always admired. On the wire fence along the pavement, the morning glory with its cerulean-blue flowers is in full bloom. On their porch, jasmine planted in a pot is studded with white flowers that drape themselves languorously over branches that catch the light from the midday sun and shine like a swarm of butterflies. On the side and to the back of the house, the garden is full of rabbit-ear irises, rose bushes, lupins, kumquat, plum and apple trees and a number of established olive trees. The seating area rests on the exposed rock amid the flowering plants by a drystone wall.

I have often been for dinner here. It is a veritable paradise. And yet this oasis is slated to be destroyed. Soon the bulldozers

will get to work, a large hole will be dug and an ugly multi-storey building will be constructed by the investor who has bought the land and wants to evict my two friends. Negotiations were protracted and bitter as he expressed resentment that, despite the law, he – a local – should be having to compensate foreigners for leaving land that is now his. He has not the slightest appreciation that these two women have done more in the service of justice in Palestine than he ever could, as he was busy making the money which he is now using to buy and destroy an attractive house and render Ramallah so much less pleasant. I stand by the metal gate, enjoying the scent that fills the air, and bid farewell to another of the old Ramallah houses and gardens. If this process continues only a shrinking minority of households will have a garden.

The tenants' law is a relic from the time when there were few houses available and it gave maximum protection to the tenant, though this did not apply to foreigners. Only in the last few years has it become possible for a landlord to raise the rent of new tenancies. Old tenants became like owners and so held on to their lodgings. To evict a tenant, the new owner would have to pay a lot in compensation. Many of the old houses with gardens are occupied by long-term tenants who are still holding on, but they are often old or dying, widows or unmarried daughters, with the rest of their family either already dead or long since emigrated to the US. If the new owner is not in a hurry to get returns for his investment, he waits for the tenants to die so he can acquire the property without paying compensation.

The streets with the flowering jacarandas are mainly lined with tall blocks of apartments, occasionally punctuated by those lingering single-floor stone houses roofed with red tiles, their gardens surrounded by drystone walls, that are dwarfed by the high-rises all around them. I lament the changing nature of this city, remembering how Ramallah used to have the charm and atmosphere of the mountain villages of Lebanon. Most of the pine trees have now been replaced by a kind of ficus brought in from Israel that is inappropriate for the city's harsh winters. The jacarandas that flower so gloriously in late spring lose their leaves and remain bare the entire winter.

Except for unhappy thoughts like these, my stroll is pleasant, but when I look at my watch I realise it is time to start making my way to the office.

Walking back, my thoughts turn to the many emails I receive from owners of old houses now living in the US who have sold their family homes, only to regret it later. In one of these the owner informed me that she had 'become aware that an historic family property in Ramallah, which was sold under dubious circumstances, is now slated for demolition despite the historical preservation law. I found out about it on a Facebook post from Riwaq [the centre for the conservation of cultural heritage] I am wondering if it may be possible to halt the destruction of this house as it is an important part of my family.'

Earlier, a friend who was planning to sell their family home but did not want the buyer to demolish it had written: 'Another call for help. I'm concerned, more petrified, that our house will be relegated to a pile of rubble once it gets sold sometime in the future. It was one of the first contemporary villas, if not the first, in the area. My father put his blood, sweat, tears and hard work (literally), in building this gem of a house. Do we have any legal recourse in preventing the greediness of any buyer from destroying it? It's a nightmare that keeps playing in my mind and definitely heartbreaking. It means the physical eradication of my childhood and life in Ramallah. Please advise.'

I felt for her, though I could respond only by pointing

out that it is not possible to do anything because we have no law preventing the destruction of historic buildings. Even if we did, a house such as her family's would not qualify as historical. It is only meaningful to those who have a history in it. I would not be able to do anything to stop the demolition. If she really cared about this house why did she want to sell it in the first place?

On Friends Street I encounter a long queue of traffic going up to Main Street, where my office is. I edge carefully along the street, which is lined with cars parked illegally, some double-parked. Pedestrians walk by not paying any attention to the cars, deeply involved in speaking or texting on their phones. It is getting hot now, the air warmed by the midday sun and the car fumes. On school days this street gets even more crowded. At the end of the school day parents drive to private schools to pick up their children. Every weekday this creates traffic jams on Ramallah streets. In the 1950s and 1960s we all walked to school and had a greater chance to observe and take in so much on our way there and back home again than present-day kids have.

To my left I can see the old familiar school gateposts, built in 1930. In the early 1950s, on a plot that has now been built up, there used to be a large and attractive tent where the aunt of my schoolmate Wedad Marouf lived. I never went inside, but my mother always said it was the most beautiful tent she had ever seen and that she liked visiting the family. They had lost their home in Ramle in the Nakba and refused to live in squalor, so they strove to make their tent as attractive as possible. Of the six children, only one daughter, Wedad's mother, now in her eighties, is still living in Ramallah, with two of her sons and their families.

In Ramle the father had owned a grocery shop. After the massacre by Jewish forces at Deir Yassin on 9 April 1948, he brought his wife, their three daughters and three sons to Ramallah because he was afraid for their safety. He remained in Ramle until it became too dangerous, then he also left. The family lived at the Anglican church house for a while until they found a place to rent. But after a few months they were unable to afford that. They asked the priest, who owned land across from the Friends School, whether they could squat on the plot and live in a tent there.

The mother planted the ground outside with stocks, snap-dragons and dahlias, which I could see from the street as I walked to and from school. The father roasted peanuts and every day would drag a cart heaped with nuts up that steep hill, then stand at the corner of Friends Street to sell them. He had been roasting nuts at his grocery in Ramle and continued to do so in Ramallah. One night when it snowed they had a *kanoon* (metal grill for heating that uses coal) lit in the tent. The mother woke up and found everyone drowsy and sluggish because of carbon monoxide. She got them outside and they revived. After their narrow escape from gas poisoning, they asked permission to build a room with bricks. They divided it into different quarters and lived there. The toilet remained outside.

One brother now lives in Brazil and another in the US; one sister lived and died in Wales, and another went to Australia, where the parents also immigrated, dying there. Wedad's mother is the only one to have stayed in Ramallah. Her husband had the town's sole flower shop and her son owns the Snowbar garden restaurant.

Mass emigration to the US was made easier once it was possible to get a visa if one had a brother settled there. Knowledge of English, which the Friends School provided, was another inducement. In the 1950s it became like an unstoppable stream, with Ramallah losing most of its original inhabitants. According to the 1997 census, refugees accounted for some 60 per cent of the city's population.

From the top of the hill at the end of Friends Street I can

see how busy Ramallah is now, how chaotic and noisy. Over fifty years the sounds of the town have completely changed, becoming so much louder and more unpleasant. When I heard the artist Emily Jacir's sound installation at the opening of the Palestinian Museum in Birzeit, I was reminded of how, before the Israeli occupation imprisoned us in the West Bank, we would hear taxi drivers in the centre of town calling for passengers 'to Jerusalem, to Amman, to Beirut'.

Shop owners had a habit of keeping caged songbirds just outside their shops. The birds would chirrup most of the day, making the owner proud. With the felling of the pine trees lining the city streets by Israeli soldiers – on security grounds, they said – one can no longer hear birds in the trees. Their song has been replaced by the noise of traffic. There were also a number of men-only coffee shops where young men played pool, which we called *billyardoo*. Ramallah was a poor town with few places of entertainment. Bored with nothing to do, young men would stroll in the streets, swaying their arms with their little fingers linked. They were usually from the surrounding villages, where the practice was thought to indicate the strong bond of male friendship. Shop owners sat outside their shops on low stools in the sun, twirling cigarettes between their yellowed fingers. They would use hand gestures to communicate with each other from opposite sides of the street, along which only a few cars passed. Occasionally a driver would stop to chat, keeping one hand on the gear stick and the other, usually tanned, out of the open window. The shop owner would lean down, poke his head in the car and start a conversation with the driver. They had the time to tell each other stories and greet passers-by. Rather than use the indicator, taxi drivers would extend their hand out of the window to signal that they were making a turn.

On the evenings when the band at the Grand Hotel wasn't playing we sat in the pine garden of our old house. Apart from the occasional honk, there would be utter silence. On warm summer days we heard crickets and the occasional braying of a mule drawing a cart or the clunky old bus making its rounds. We didn't have television until the late 1950s and we rarely turned on the radio in our house. Children played outside the house – one could often hear their shouts as they played marbles or the popular game of seven stones. The streets were dominated by men. Every once in a while a woman would pass by, either the barber's attractive wife, walking so straight, her hair tied in a chignon, or our neighbours' young daughter with her flowing auburn hair. A hush would descend on the street, everything coming to a halt as all eyes turned to look.

Until the late 1980s, except for older women none wore the headscarf. It is different now. These days a large number of women cover their hair and some also wear the full-length traditional Islamic dress. It often makes me feel as though I no longer recognise where I am. It's not that I mind the headscarf; it's just that it makes me yearn for the time when nationalism provided the public with a sense of identity. Now that the ✓ nationalist project has failed, it has been replaced by religion.

As I pass through the crowded Main Street someone inadvertently pushes me then immediately apologises, calling me *Haj*, a term of respect that, when I was growing up, was reserved for someone who had gone on the pilgrimage to Mecca. In the past people used other, non-religious terms, such as *Khawaja*, Mr or *Ustaz*, but not *Haj*. The first time I was called this, a few years ago, I was surprised. Now it is used to address all men my age, whether Christian or Muslim.

Just before reaching the office I pass Abu Iskandar's famous *shawarma* place, where I used to go with my grandmother. In the renovated stopfront I can see Iskandar the son, now as portly as his father used to be, sitting by the window, his hefty arms folded in a similar pose. I greet him, though I haven't bought a sandwich from him since I stopped eating meat in 1991. The all too familiar and still-enticing smell wafts by my nose as I make my way up to the office.

Nine

As I walk up the stairs to my office I see by the door the old sign: 'Aziz and Fuad Shehadeh Law Office'. It has been hanging on the wall, at the top of the stairs, from before I joined, thirty-seven years ago.

I was number 176 on the list of registered lawyers when I began practising law. There was no Palestinian Bar Association then. Almost as many lawyers had joined the longest-lasting, disastrous lawyers' strike, which began right after the occupation in protest at the illegal annexation by Israel of East Jerusalem and lasted for some quarter of a century, achieving nothing. As long as they remained on strike, the lawyers received a monthly stipend from the Jordanian Bar Association. Those who refused to join were disbarred by the association, to which all Palestinian lawyers then belonged. A new lawyer had the option of registering either with the Jordanian Bar and joining the strike or with the Israeli military and becoming qualified to appear before the local courts administered by them. I was confronted with the choice whether or not to join the strike. I had no doubt as to what I should do. I wanted to be a practising lawyer who used the law to serve the cause of human rights. Now there are over 3,500 lawyers registered with the Palestinian Bar Association, which was established in the wake of the Oslo Accords.

After completing my studies and before leaving London, I had two suits made, one in striped grey and another in black. I also bought a barrister's gown. The suits have since worn out, but the gown still hangs in the office although I rarely use it now. I was determined to play the part and do my best for the practice. Until the agreement was signed between the PLO and Israel in Oslo, I continued to see the usefulness of law in serving the struggle for liberation from the occupation. That event put an end to my aspirations. Then my public work seemed futile and my writing came into the ascendance.

I have never regretted studying law, but when I turned fifty I became curious about another possible direction my life could have taken had I stayed at the Sri Aurobindo Ashram in Pondicherry, which I visited in 1974, and joined Auroville. I was twenty-three then and enjoyed many aspects of life in the ashram, especially the communal kitchen and the ritual of eating together simple food, which seemed to agree with me. I had never felt better. During my stay at the ashram I heard a lot about Auroville, a universal city being built by idealists from around the world who wanted to explore new ways of communal living. I longed to be part of that ambitious project, but I had to leave India without ever visiting Auroville. News arrived that my mother was ill. My departure was so swift that I left behind all the clothes I had acquired there, bar one salmon-coloured cotton shirt which I held on to until it became so worn it could not be mended. That city in India remained in my mind as the unreachable nirvana. Now, at fifty, I was determined to visit the place and see what I had missed.

On arriving at Auroville, I saw that the new city resembled

an Israeli settlement, with the difference that it was built around the Matrimandir, a meditation dome for the practitioners of integral yoga based on the philosophy and practice of Sri Aurobindo and the Mother, Mirra Alfassa. It is situated in what is called the Peace temple, which is dedicated to the Mother, who was the inspiration behind Auroville. When I got there, I saw long queues of tourists all wanting to visit the golden dome. I stood with them in silence and observed the area around me. It was inhabited mainly by foreigners and survived in the midst of abject poverty. Many of the inhabitants were totally self-involved, convinced that they were serving higher ideals while being totally detached from those among whom they lived, and who they sometimes employed as cheap labour. Some people had left their own highly developed societies and moved to Auroville simply because they could afford it. They made themselves believe they were leading moral lives, carrying out a new experiment in socialist living.

Before leaving, I visited the bakery and bought some bread, then went to the gift shop, where I bought a lampshade and a necktie produced by Aurovillians – two mementoes which I still keep of the place to which I once thought I would dedicate my life.

Knowing how much I dislike meetings, I would never have been happy living in that collective environment, where meetings were deemed necessary to take decisions on various aspects of communal living. Surely it was not a place for a writer who needs to be left alone in peace and quiet. It didn't take much for me to recognise that I could never have tolerated life in Auroville. I came back confirmed that I had made the right decision.

I didn't know it then, but in time it has become clear that my life was not going to be dedicated to participating in building the new ideal society but in exposing the ills inflicted upon

my own society. Not in the distant yonder, but in the dirt, pain
and suffering of the here and now. And so, between my work
at the law office and Al Haq, I managed to keep myself busy
with trying to discover and expose Israeli policies regarding the
occupied territories and the changes in the law being made by
the military authorities. I was working assiduously to see the
total picture, keeping ahead of the occupier, figuring out what
was happening and writing about it in the hope of putting a
stop to these violations. With the vast increase in Jewish settlements and the intolerable stifling of Palestinian society, what
good has it done? In the chaotic crowded streets filled with calls
to prayer, it feels more like we are praying for our sins, acknowl-
edging our defeat and pleading for forgiveness.

My busiest years as a lawyer at the office were after the Oslo
deal was struck. Then I had plenty of legal work for larger
projects than our office had ever handled. This was fortuitous,
because I needed money to build our house so I could shelter
from the chaos and at the end of the day return to a tranquil
orderly place. Meanwhile the hard work and long hours at the
office provided a perfect distraction from the gloomy outlook
that the Oslo Accords projected for our future.

Our office was not far from where the District Court came
to be located. When I was young I used to accompany my father
to the District Court in Jerusalem. This was a new building
erected by Jordan when it governed eastern Jerusalem. Father
was proud of the impressive structure and would rush up the
wide stairs to argue his cases there before the Arab judges. But
when I began my practice that building had been taken over by
Israel and was being used as the Israeli District Court. What
had served as the Ramallah vegetable market was used to house
our Palestinian courts for all levels of the judiciary from the
magistrates' courts to the High Court. I never thought about

the blow to father, who then had to make do with arguing his cases before these shabby courts.

So much has happened at this office that I am now entering. Happy times, tense times, successes and failures. Despite everything, I have never regretted staying in Ramallah and working as a lawyer. It has not always been easy to live here or to work in the family firm. My uncle lost his sight. First he lost sight in one eye in a traffic accident while on his way to court in Jenin and then he lost the second eye due to diabetes. My father was murdered after leaving his office on a foggy December evening in 1985, by a thug who had squatted on church property whom my father was trying to evict. As a collaborator working for the military, the assassin was never pursued by the Israeli police. We endured the first, then the second Intifada and several wars, before and after, including the reinvasion of Ramallah in 2002. Fortunately, the office was spared and was never broken into by the army.

Over the years the office expanded, with two of my cousins joining my uncle and myself. Later, other partners were added to our team. Now it is considered among the largest and most prestigious law firms in Palestine. My father would be proud. The latest recruit is my nephew Aziz, the same boy of seven to whom I showed the tank near my home, now grown into a bright young man determined to make his life here, despite the difficulties of occupation.

When I arrive at the office, I find he has been here since nine this morning and will be staying until late in the evening. Like his grandfather, he is diligent and hard-working. He will fill his grandfather's place admirably; even his handwriting is neat like his.

I have done my best to guide him to become a good lawyer and avoid the mistakes I have made. Yet when I see him at the office I am overcome by conflicting emotions. I have managed to hand over to him the office I inherited from my father, which my colleagues and I have kept prosperous and well established, but I cannot spare him the suffering from an ever-more tenacious occupation and grim future, much as I feel confident that he will find his own way of coping and resisting. He has come back, hasn't he?

After my father died I refused to use his office and stayed where I was in the small room next to his. It was months before I felt able to inherit his room. But it was not without pain. As I enter it today I think of him, as I invariably do every time I come to the office.

My one-thirty meeting did not take much time. After working as a lawyer for thirty-seven years, I have learned the skill of how to be expeditious. Afterwards I responded to a few emails, then sat with my colleagues to discuss the issues they were handling. They wanted my opinion on a number of legal matters and asked me to review some letters they had drafted concerning sensitive issues. There was nothing urgent that couldn't wait for another day, but I thought I would spend the rest of the afternoon at the office, going through my pending work. However, at that point my secretary came to tell me that an old client of mine had just called, asking whether I was going to be at the office this afternoon because he wanted to pass by and see me. I have known this man for many years and have promised myself I will never handle another of his seemingly interminable cases. I told her to say I was leaving. I know him well enough to feel sure that he would soon be appearing at my office anyhow, to catch me before I left. So, to make sure that I avoided an unpleasant encounter with him, I sped out of the office.

On leaving, I turn left on Main Street and begin walking down Post Office Street. There is a car park to my left which, during the reinvasion of Ramallah in the spring of 2002, contained five Israeli tanks shooting randomly in all directions. The house we moved to in 1967 was at the southern end of the car park. The back of the nearby Midan Building is still pockmarked by the shells that were fired at it. Seeing it brought back memories of that sad time during Ramallah's most recent ordeal.

My first thought was that I would continue down this street, then turn left on to Jaffa Road and make a long detour home through Batn Al Hawa Road. But after reaching halfway down the street, one of my favourites as it is lined with huge plane trees, something – perhaps force of habit – draws me to the street of the last abode of my parents. I turn left towards the flat that the family rented after the 1967 war. When I get there, I pause and look up at the third floor, where we lived. In the garden the orange trumpet vine that the owner planted years ago is flourishing and has spread all over the outer wall.

When we moved there, Nabiha Salah, a widow, was living alone across the street in a house that she owned. She had a basement room which she rented. One day, soon after the beginning of the occupation in 1967, a single, clean-looking man knocked on her door and asked to rent the empty room. She did not recognise the man and didn't think of asking. She was in need of money. It was Yasser Arafat, who was on the run. He didn't stay long. The Israeli army, which was pursuing him, soon discovered where he was staying and came after him. They banged on Nabiha's door, but she refused to open it.

Speaking with an American accent, which she had acquired during six years living there as a child and which she had managed to retain, she told them, 'Go away. I'm an American citizen.'

They were not impressed and threatened, 'If you don't open up we'll break down the door.'

Meanwhile Arafat had made his way out of the basement, crossed the road and hidden in our garage, where he waited for the army to leave before going in search of another hideout. This first visit at the start of Arafat's life of struggle was not the last. Some twenty-five years later he returned to Ramallah after the signing of the Oslo Accords, when for a few years he acted like the president of a virtual state. Following the second Intifada, the Israeli army invaded his headquarters in March 2002 and kept him under siege for six months. His last abode, the small room in which he was holed up before he died, his 'bunker', is the only part of the old Mandate-built Muqata'a that is preserved. It forms part of the Yasser Arafat Museum dedicated to his life and his memory. How could I have known then that the short, wiry man who rented a room from our eccentric neighbour would come to dominate our lives and that our small city would become the de facto capital of a strange virtual state, with a museum devoted to him as its founder, where visiting heads of state would stop, his life memorialised and honoured in our city?

When I lived with my parents in this rented flat after the 1967 war, I was so full of words. At night words would bubble out of my mouth during sleep, as my brother Samer, with whom I shared a bedroom, would complain. At that time, words also came out in profuse lyrical writing that pushed back the world around me and kept me alive in my own alternative place. I mainly listened to the reel of words running in my head and was not so attentive to those around me. It was partly my way of rebelling, to shake away the world and live in one of my own making.

When my mother died, many years after she was widowed, Samer and I gave up this flat. Now I cannot go there and visit. The owner has raised the outer wall, which fortunately obstructs the view of the garage driveway where my father lay in a pool of blood. But I could still see the third-floor glass balcony on which I often sat with my father discussing office work, while mother rebuked us, saying, 'No shop talk here, please.'

Not long before my father died, he reviewed his savings with me, assuring me that he could live off them to the end of his days and would not need my help. Whatever was left would be mine. And yet I was not relieved, appreciative or impressed. I wondered why he was telling me this: was it to win my sympathy for approaching the end of his life? I was not interested in his assets and had decided I would disinherit myself. Nor did I appreciate that he was organising all his papers so that there would be no confusion when he died. He told me, 'I am seventy-three. How much longer have I got to live?' And again I dismissed this as old man's talk. Why was it so between us?

Now, many years later, I know that it was neither money nor material possessions that were important. These I could do without. What I needed, and have been seeking all these years since his death, was proof and acknowledgement of his love. And, as I have lately discovered, his friendship.

Why had I hardened my heart so? Because I was too proud, arrogant and ambitious, so much so that I didn't want to settle for these material comforts and traditional relations? Wasn't I going to do extraordinary things and go beyond these norms and conventions? I was not going to be merely an obedient son, anxious about the future, just like all the others. Didn't he realise that I was special and had great ambitions? That I was going to forge a different and unique future?

In a culture that expected blind respect from son to father, where a son may not judge or disobey his father, I sought to be different. I defined respect as arguing back and finding my own way, and making this known rather than believing that concealing such rejection and rebellion was kinder. It cannot have been easy for my father living among others who saw my manner as disrespectful and utterly misguided. In his own way, my father had tried to tell me about the trials of old age, but I did not listen. Perhaps had I done so I would be better prepared for what I'm going through now, when I'm closer to his age then. To my regret and loss, I was blind to his ageing journey, which is perhaps the plight of everyone getting to that age.

I have achieved some of my ambitions. And yet more than anything, I yearn for him to have been a part of my success, to acknowledge it and celebrate it with me. Perhaps because in large part I had wanted success in order to win him over. As a boy I used to go to my father when he was standing by the sink shaving and announce that I came first in my class. He would not say anything, just smile approvingly. That smile meant the world to me. I never ever wanted to disappoint him.

Human rights activism was my alternative arena and from this he was absent, or rather I absented him. It enabled me to believe that I was more moral, more egalitarian, less elitist, serving all society and not just our clients, and a part of the political struggle on my own terms. Al Haq was my alternative workplace, where I made my own decisions. I didn't want my father's interference or censure. My work in human rights led me to be secretive. I didn't want to alarm him by making him aware of our various campaigns against Israeli policies. I didn't want him to worry. This made him suspicious of what I was doing and who I really was. Much as I wanted my father to love me I didn't allow him to father me.

He and I had such different personalities and interests, but since I didn't allow myself to be attentive to him or conscious of what he had to do to survive, I didn't understand how his character was a reaction to the forces which, in time, I too would have to face. I never took into consideration his age. There were a number of passions that we shared, such as music. Why could we have not enjoyed these together? I know now that I have much to be grateful to him for and that I never thanked him or acknowledged his contribution to who I became or what I was able to accomplish.

When Niall McDermott, the Secretary General of the International Commission of Jurists, came from Geneva to visit us in Ramallah after we had established Al Haq, it was Nabeel, one of father's trainees, whom we invited to have dinner with Niall. He had become one of the prominent young lawyers who smoked a pipe, wore a three-piece suit and looked like a caricature of a barrister. He sat there at the head of the table and ordered a *nergila*. He was utterly unconcerned about the state of human rights and saw no role for himself as a lawyer in the struggle we were so passionate about. Like many others, he was in the legal profession only for the money.

Now when I recall the list of guests at that dinner I realise that father was not among them. At the time I did not give any thought to how he must have felt to have been excluded. But then I was so concerned that this project had to be separate from the office, and from my father, that I did not even consider it. I feared that my father would be too cynical or dominant. It is only now that I'm able to face the truth that my project in human rights was conducted to distinguish myself from him. My success in my various projects won me praise from many quarters, yet one word of praise from him would have been worth the world.

I totally misread my parents' midlife crisis. How could I have understood when I was so self-absorbed? For many years, every time I passed this building I thought of how my parents had died here. But then it was also here that they lived the happiest years of their lives. It is more a reflection on me that I insist on remembering only the sad events and not the happy ones. These were the years when they travelled and had friends. They knew how to live well. They both worked hard and yet were good at holidays and hosting parties. They had a good life. After mother died I could see only the sad parts of her life and this coloured everything, cancelling out what had gone before, the happier days.

But now is the time to remember their happy times. They moved into this house fifty years ago, at the start of the occupation. It made my mother so happy to move out of the old, cold house that never saw the sun and was difficult to heat. She would sit on the glass balcony which was flooded with sunlight and say, 'It cannot be better than this.' From that balcony we could see the outskirts of Jerusalem. My father was then hopeful of Palestinian statehood, despite everything, and was working hard for it. He had a growing number of supporters among both Israelis and Palestinians. But as Israel and the Palestinian leadership in exile fought against 'a mere state' in the West Bank, East Jerusalem and Gaza, which they dubbed 'a statelet', that hope began to dwindle and later events proved the practical futility of this happening any time soon. And now it is what most Palestinians crave.

So much happened to me in this house, not all of it happy. I was ensnared in the tragic and unresolvable tug-of-war between my mother and her mother, who insisted on visiting just when my father came home for lunch. That exaggerated irritation he expressed when *Tata* visited must have been augmented by the distressed state he was in. Once when we were driving back from Jerusalem he questioned the point of all his efforts with the law. 'Had I applied myself and worked as hard as I have in some scientific pursuit I would have got somewhere,' he confided, clearly doubting the value of the work in law and politics to which he had dedicated his life. At the time this didn't register with me: I was unable to empathise with him or appreciate his regrets.

My mother loathed her mother's ways, though she tried not to show it. But then at the end of her own life she seemed to exhibit the same behaviour towards her own children that her mother had shown her. Health issues, particularly, and mother's high blood pressure (which I too suffer from and properly managed presents no danger to life), were constantly used for emotional blackmail. I was kept on edge about the state of her health and resented being beckoned so often to be with her.

For many years, my mother seemed unable to reconcile her wish to please both her mother and her husband. I took my mother's side against my grandmother, as I took her side against my father. I became harsh and insensitive and continued to be so even when my once-beloved *Tata* was dying. Thirty-five years later, I still don't know how it would have been best to act. I am sure, however, that it was wrong of me to harden my heart, a mistake for which I've paid a heavy price. Nothing in my life has been harder to accept than realising I should have acted differently in the various family tragedies. I kept on seeing father through my mother's eyes. I was so attentive to my mother, who would not let go of me. There was a politics of alliance which I was unconscious of and I allowed myself to be recruited to her side.

Perhaps this was why I had so wanted him to 'teach' me how to shave, to openly show recognition that I was moving in status from mother's boy to father's man. But because he did not understand my need, he never did. No wonder he felt closer to my brother, Samer, who was in good health and had none of my psychological hang-ups, strange needs or vulnerability.

My parents took care of each other as family – they were practically each other's only family – but they were of different characters and temperaments. My father was ambitious and politically engaged, while my mother was uninterested and wanted nothing to do with politics, nor would she lend her support to my father in his various public activities. She would often repeat what her father used to say: 'I have enough troubles of my own.' She also had her own mother to take care of, who had absolutely no one else around and was a difficult woman. When the regime made my father's life difficult and it would have made more sense for them to leave Jordan and emigrate to the US in the 1950s, they didn't. There, my father's energy could have found an outlet and been better utilised, and this would have made him happier and more fulfilled. But my mother could not leave her mother behind, or take her along. She was always torn between her mother and her husband and often the strain was excessive and emotionally debilitating. It tore her apart. Three years after my grandmother died, my mother was widowed.

At her moment of great distress for the loss of her husband, my mother rejected me. After I returned from my travels to find my father killed, I rushed to comfort her. She did not want my embrace. I thought I could offer her some solace, but it was not to be. Only later could I understand and accept that her loss, as she experienced it in her solitude, was so complete that no one, not even I, could ease it. Much as I tried to get her out of her deep depression and mourning, which lasted for many years, perhaps to the end of her life, I could never succeed. Seeing her like this, so distant, so unapproachable, broke my heart.

I often came from the office down that same Post Office Street to have lunch with her and keep her company. She was depressed for so long. One kind of depression while my father was alive and her mother harassed her, and another much worse after he died. I was caught in the middle, never able to resolve anything yet tied and emotionally entangled. I struggled to be free, to be away from it all, but barely succeeded.

After all these years, I feel sympathy for my mother, who was sent away to boarding school and not given attention and love by her mother. I understand that she so wanted to do it differently with her own children that she ended up stifling us.

It was only years after his death that I came to understand my father's mood swings and the depth of despair he felt before he died. He was dismayed by how the Palestinian leadership was acting and felt they were losing precious time, allowing Israel to proceed with its colonial project. He understood that as the years passed the Israelis were becoming only more right wing and less inclined to make peace with the Palestinians. He could see how quickly the settlements were being built and Israelis encouraged to move to them. I came to understand the effect his disillusionment had on his life because it was not unlike how I had felt after our leadership signed the Oslo Accords. But I had my writing to consume my energy. Father didn't have this alternative.

I do not presume to understand the relationship between my parents. It was complicated, as with most married couples. They were at the same time family and adversaries, attracted and repelled, yet passionate about each other at different times.

A few months before my father was murdered I was having lunch with my parents. My father was in a bad mood and he was putting my mother down. I tried to intervene by supporting her when my father snapped at me, saying, 'You don't understand anything.' I deeply regret never asking him what he meant. What was it that I did not understand? Could it be that he knew I viewed my mother uncritically, that I was under her spell and did not realise how difficult it was for him to live with a person as anxious as her?

I can see my father walking energetically down the garden path to the staircase to climb up to our flat. He doesn't look at the garden. Unlike me, he was never interested in plants or flowers. I inherited that interest from my grandmother. I felt a strong desire to call after him to stop and unburden my heart to him:

In my sixty-sixth year I've come back to visit where you last lived to tell you how much I miss knowing and befriending you. You used to be so tense at the law office when we worked together and you made life difficult for me. Only after experiencing the tribulations of getting older have I been able to understand the state of rage you exhibited in those last years of your life which distanced us even more.

When you most needed me to cheer you up, boost your morale and give you hope, I was judgemental and competitive. I could only think of myself. You had given me so much and were tolerant of my wayward behaviour when I was young, yet I could not reciprocate. I wanted you out of the way. I wanted you away from the office because it would be easier for me like that.

I thought the obvious answer would be for you to leave, to retire. I told you so, not aware how cruel I sounded. How brutal and unfeeling I was, asking you to retire at the time when you most needed to work and keep busy to manage your apprehensions. How could I have known that what you needed most was the assurance that you were still valued, rather than being shunned?

Now that I've achieved some of my ambitions and almost reached the age you were when you died, I appreciate that old age is a peculiar state of its own, like being in a liminal space. And this has helped me understand you as I never could before. I come back on this visit as an older, more emotionally mature man. Only now do I begin to understand what you lived through and how well you dealt with it. And how insensitive I was to your attempts to alert me to what was happening to you so that I would be prepared when the time came for me to go through similar experiences.

Your voice was muted by louder voices. It wasn't, as

I've always assumed, only in political matters, because of your unpopular views, that you were silenced. I too was guilty of trying for the longest time to silence you, to my deep regret now, because more than anything I grieve at having lost the opportunity to enjoy your company and your friendship.

I used to think that you and I had such different temperaments we could never get along. Now I realise how fundamentally similar we were and how much of what I became I acquired from you.

I was not there to protect you in your moment of great need. Perhaps I could have saved you. Perhaps it would not have happened had I been there with you, standing by your side. But I was away working on another of my human rights missions. During the Intifada I had the illusion that it would be possible to achieve personal justice for you through the collective struggle. It wasn't to be.

As I stand on the street below and look up at the glass balcony, how I wish I could climb the stairs and go in with you and sit there together in the sun. I have so much I would like to tell you, not least how much I respect, admire and love you. And how anguished I feel at failing you.

As was his habit, my father rushed away before I could say more, and I was left alone on the pavement feeling slightly unburdened of what had remained unsaid for many years.

Ten

Leaving our old family home, I cross the street to look at one of the few remaining drystone walls. Constructed without the use of mortar by one of the experts in this dying skill, with stones skilfully selected and placed to ensure strength and durability, it demarcated the land above it from the pavement, a rare example of the most enduring method of defining territory. A pleasant sight and a reminder of what all garden walls in Ramallah used to be like. It stood alone, yet not long ago it was one of a series of walls that covered the entire hillside. Where once sheep grazed the area is now entirely built up. The sound of sheep and birds has been replaced by car horns. I pass my hand over its age-worn stones, green and black with lichen, as in a farewell, feeling certain it will not be there for long.

I have just left the street named after my paternal grandfather, Bolous Shehadeh. He was a poet and the editor of *Mirat es Shark* (*Mirror of the East*), a newspaper published during the British Mandate. Though originally from Ramallah, he left when he was a young man and resided for the rest of his life in Jerusalem, where my father was raised. Like me, he was a short man; perhaps this is why the municipality chose a short street to name after him. Nearby was the Bardouni Building, a new four-storey structure with a glass front, previously the site of a lovely garden restaurant where I often took my mother for meals. The new Ramallah buildings feature many of these façades, evidence that another stone-throwing Intifada is far from people's minds and expectations, though maybe now they're just using bulletproof glass.

I turn and continue walking up Jaffa Street towards the shabby Midan Es Sa'ah (clock tower roundabout), now called Yasser Arafat Square, in the centre of town. A sculpture has been placed there, showing a young man climbing towards the Palestinian flag, which is permanently hoisted. As I looked at it, I wondered how many had died through electrification or were shot by Israeli army snipers as they tried to raise the flag on an electricity pole in the Intifada days, and whether they had died senselessly. Yet raising a flag then was an act of resistance that cannot now be frowned upon. Could such thoughts, as I look at this memorial, be similar to what old-timers in Berlin feel when they see the remnants of the wall that caused the death of dear ones while it separated the two parts of their city? But they succeeded in removing the wall, while our struggle goes on.

From where I stand I can see Awda (the Return) Street, where Muhamad, one of the sons of Faik, a former employee who for a long time was a typist at our law office, was killed by an Israeli sniper as he fought in the second armed Intifada. Perpendicular to that street, reaching all the way south to the Water Works Department, is Hanna Mikhael Street, named after the son of one of the Ramallah families and a Harvard University graduate. In 1969 he left a promising academic career at one of the top US universities to join the PLO, first in Jordan and then in Lebanon. In July 1976, during the Lebanese civil war, he and nine of his comrades and two sailors disappeared while on their way by sea to the besieged Palestinian camps in northern Lebanon. To this day, his exact fate remains unknown. I can imagine that, like so many others, Faik and his family must avoid areas around Ramallah where loved ones were killed. The father was a dedicated parent and a hard-working man. He had two jobs, full-time at the Health Department and part-time as a typist at our office. That was before word-processing. One mistake with a legal document and he had to retype the whole page, as many times as necessary. He was already employed when I joined the office. Short and stocky, with a moustache, he would sit for hours in front of the manual typewriter without moving, diligently punching away at the keys in Arabic or English. I remember how he described his wife when he got married as 'a healthy woman'. He did not say beautiful or attractive. He seemed more impressed with her plump red cheeks and was obviously thinking of the children she would give him. He was relieved when I built a house. When I asked why, he said, 'Now I know you will not emigrate. You'll stay here.' It was an indication that he never believed in my commitment to Palestine. We were friends. When I tripped, fell and broke my nose during a busy time at the office, he took me to hospital to get me checked over.

Faik was a refugee from 1948, living in the Kalandia refugee camp, close to Jerusalem. But he did not want his four boys getting involved in politics, which is the fate of most of those who grow up in the highly politicised atmosphere of the camp. So he worked hard to buy a house outside the camp and moved his family there. But things did not turn out as he hoped. His eldest son, Amjad, began his activism when he was only fourteen. I defended him in the military court in Nablus when he was charged with throwing stones at an Israeli jeep. The hearing took place in the attractive Ottoman building that also served as a jail, which was sadly demolished in the late 1990s by the Palestinian

Authority. I was proud to be able to get him a lenient sentence and released from detention upon payment of a small fine. But as we were leaving the court, I heard Amjad shouting from the window of the detention centre where he was being held, warning his father not to pay. This was before the first Intifada.

During the Intifada I was at the office with Faik when the Israeli-appointed mayor of nearby Beitunia, against whom the office had raised a civil case, came and began threatening me. He ended up beating Faik, who tried to defend me. It wasn't too serious and yet Faik insisted that he get an apology and compensation, not through the courts, because with the perpetrator's close connection to the Israeli administration it would be impossible to get a favourable decision, but through the traditional reconciliation process. He would not rest until they made a *sulha* (truce) and he was awarded compensation. This was how it was during the occupation. Without police or proper courts, the only protection came from one's extended family and supporters and Faik had the camp and Fatah supporters behind him, even though he had moved out.

I realised the big difference between our standing when one day during the Intifada I was delivering books to a friend. I was in my red Peugeot, the very first car I ever owned, which was a present from my father after I qualified as a lawyer. I drove through Manara in the centre of town and down Chicken Street, where the Ramallah courts were. As I passed I remember hearing a loud whistle but paid no attention to it. I parked my car on the slope next to my friend's house, but just as I climbed out I heard a loud rumbling noise. I looked up and saw the trailer of a truck that had become disconnected hurtling down the road straight at me. I considered getting back into my red car and driving away. Fortunately, I didn't, because all too soon the rushing trailer, which had gained speed, crashed into my car and rammed it into an electricity pole. Sparks flew from the car as it shot down the slope, finally coming to rest against a low wall, just short of falling into the garden of a house below street level. The car was a total write-off. But at least I wasn't in it and no one got hurt.

The owner of the truck turned out to be a collaborator. Nothing could be done. It would have been futile to attempt to get compensation from him through the courts. I was never sure whether it was an accident or if someone deliberately unhitched the trailer in an attempt to kill someone. I never found out. There were no police then. The incident that could have killed me was never investigated. I knew better than to pursue the collaborators, but that incident made me realise how unprotected I was. I didn't dwell on my own powerlessness, because what mattered then was the larger collective struggle that would change everything.

During the first Intifada we all acted in solidarity. At first I was such a novice. I remember the time I went to visit a client, the Fatah activist Ziad Abu Ayn, at the high-security Negev Desert prison called Nafha. I was with his brother, Mahmoud. It was my first time there. We had a good session with Ziad and as we were leaving he leapt up and hugged me, which I thought was his way of thanking me for coming all that way to visit him. Then he gave me a kiss on the mouth and stuck his tongue in. When he withdrew it I felt something slimy in my mouth. I was horrified and disgusted by his behaviour.

As soon as we left, I took from my mouth what looked like a small capsule. I held it between two fingers and showed it to Mahmoud. 'Look what Ziad left in my mouth,' I told him. He asked me to give it to him, saying this was a *kabsuleh* (capsule). It was the first time I had heard of such a thing. Mahmoud took it, removed the plastic wrap and began to unfurl the thin, translucent paper with its tiny writing. Unwittingly I had participated in my first experience of smuggling messages from prison.

The time of hope and solidarity we felt then was so different from what followed the Oslo Accords, when the huge sums of money pouring in acted like scissors, tearing society apart and creating polarisation as never before. Prior to Oslo no Palestinian was willing to blow himself up to kill enemy civilians. The political factions involved in the struggle were mainly secular. The fight was against Israeli soldiers and settlers, the stone against the gun. As I stand in the Midan, looking up at the sculpture intended to memorialise a past struggle, memories of how the town looked during the first Intifada return to me.

Then, in the late 1980s, the public spaces in the city came to have a different feel. Whenever the army arrived, the streets were filled with warning whistles. There were no mobile phones or social media. Masked youth roamed the streets, distributing leaflets with instructions for the next mode of struggle. The 'I' changed to 'we' as the public began to express its collective will to liberate the land from occupation, taking great risks. The shuttered shops became our pride, the forced opening by soldiers a personal insult and attack on our collective will. The heroism and solidarity of the shop owners was carefully monitored and commended. No doubt some went along reluctantly, fearful of reprisals if they didn't, refusing to share the collective hope and wanting only to be left alone to get on with their business. But for the majority, these years are often recalled as the best years of their lives. This is especially true now, when there is a dearth of hope. Going up and down the streets then, one felt oneself on the battlefield. Some streets were closed by the military, others by our own barricades. The city space was no longer a neutral marketplace but an arena of struggle.

All this made me feel a closer affinity with the people of my town than I have ever felt before or since. The occupation was an equaliser. It limited everyone's freedom without discrimination and brought us all together as one, rich and poor, men and women. I interviewed the owner of the shop at the corner, Heliopolis Fashion, which sold fancy wedding gowns and evening dresses. The burglars who had come in the night to rob his shop were, he believed, backed by the army. I wrote about this for the *Jerusalem Post*, an Israeli newspaper. He appreciated this and has been my friend ever since. After that incident neighbourhood watches were organised for protection against the army. I felt proud of the brave young men and women for their courage and drive. There was a great sense of solidarity that I have never forgotten.

The shop owners shut their premises when they were called upon to do so, even when they hated it. I found I was reacting to and viewing them differently. Traditionally they are the most conservative element in society. They display their wares in order to sell them and cannot do so if they have to close. Shops whose owners hid demonstrators running from the army were sealed by the Israeli army. Generally, whatever the conditions, they endure them. They hang around, stand by their shops anticipating customers, commenting on the action.

I was struck by the degree to which the shop owners on these streets were like the chorus in a Greek tragedy. They had their own views of things, their own wisdom, and ultimately all they wanted was to be left alone to lead their lives and conduct their business. Those who got angry and undertook desperate action were not among the chorus. In the first Intifada the shop owners took part in the struggle and were in fact its backbone. Not so any more. Now they only watch the action, comment on it and rarely take part. Despite themselves, some became heroes. Then, like many viewers, they just watched the footage of the war directed against them on television, becoming observers twice-removed.

We are all garrulous and our commentary is ongoing.

We remain, we watch and we comment on the actions of the protagonists propelling the narrative line. We no longer take things into our own hands. The older ones among us are the guardians of history. We were there when the occupation first began, some when the Nakba took place. Some were around during the first Intifada and were still here when the change of guard took place and the Palestinian Authority replaced the Israeli army in the cities. The likelihood is that many of these shop owners will still be here when the Palestinian Authority is replaced by whoever comes next. The actors come and go, but the chorus remains.

After fifty years of trying, we have not succeeded in forcing Israel to end its occupation of our land. This would have required a stronger, more sustained struggle and much greater sacrifices. All we could do was to bring Israel to self-destruct. The country that occupied us half a century ago bears little resemblance to the Israel of today. By forcing them to justify the unjustifiable, that which is patently illegal, we have helped them destroy their legal system and, through their open discrimination, the rule of law and respect for international law. We have also helped destroy the socialist aspects of their system by providing them with cheap labour. We have certainly not won, but neither have they.

Having walked up to the busy Manara roundabout, with its four plastic lions, from which six roads lead to different parts of the city, I continue north towards one of them, Irsal Street, so called because it led to the four Mandate-built radio transmission towers, which had been out of commission since 1948. Once they were the first markers of the city one saw on approaching. A few years ago three were bombed to smithereens by Israel, so now only one remains. I planned to walk along Irsal and then take a left at Ayn Musbah Street back to my house. It would be a long walk of several hours but it would get me home before dark.

As I suspected, there is no public gathering or collective activity anywhere to mark the fiftieth anniversary of the occupation. Instead the centre of town is crowded mainly with young men, cars and shoppers. There is no enthusiasm for commercial strikes any more: people have to work hard to repay bank loans. With the Israeli economy dominating ours, we all have to work much harder just to keep up. Many talk into their mobile phones or use them to check stock exchange prices as they walk.

Except for the branch of the Arab Bank, which was careful to keep the same front when it, along with all the other banks that had operated before the occupation, was reopened after twenty-five years of enforced closure, most of the buildings around Manara are new, hastily built structures that sprang up immediately after the signing of the Oslo Accords.

I cross the roundabout that is busy with cars and people and, with hurried steps, walk along Irsal Street just as a Palestinian police car is passing. I notice that its windows have bars just like the Israeli military vehicles that used to roam our streets during the occupation of the city. I wonder how our police feel about having to ride in cars resembling those that our enemy had to barricade themselves in?

Fancy shopfronts line both sides of the street, which is swarming with shoppers. Two generations have been born since the first Intifada. They have no memory of how the city looked when news came that a peace deal with Israel had been struck. Most have no experience of that time at the end of the Intifada.

As long as the resistance was going on, we who were living through it did not see what had become of our city. It was only after it came to an inglorious end, when the Oslo Accord was

announced in 1993, that we began to look properly, and what
we saw was not pleasant. Anyone visiting Ramallah then would
have been shocked. Israel's rule was weakened by our persistent
struggle but we were punished and not allowed to impose an
alternative. All we could do was wait and hope for the results of
the negotiations taking place in Washington and later in Oslo.

Thinking of this now, I realise there is always a price to be
paid for every struggle. With no local authority taking care of
the city in the last years of the Intifada, it became so desolate:
grimy, darkened and tortured, like an abandoned battlefield;
dishevelled, chaotic, disorderly, crumbling, neglected and
depressed. The streets seemed to have narrowed. The Manara
roundabout was removed by Israeli soldiers, who said this was
necessary for security reasons. They then replaced the attractive
Corinthian column and the seven stone lions at its base with a
tall lamp post and the depressing sort of yellow fog light used
on highways. Many side streets were barricaded with cement
barrels and barbed wire to block the path of escaping activists.
The tarmac was pockmarked and the pine trees lining the roads
were felled, all in the name of security. The old smooth paving
stones were removed and sold to Israel to be used in antique
quarters of Israeli cities. One wall, now known as the Wall of
Blood, was smeared with the blood of young men captured
on the streets and thrown against it by soldiers. Shop awnings
were in tatters, their sides punctured by bullets. Frayed banners
hung unevenly across the street. The street of the Mikhael café,
where the Red Rose flower shop now stands, was turned into
a shoddy pedestrian area, creating havoc with traffic flows. All
of the changes were designed for maximum manoeuvrability
of army jeeps in pursuit of demonstrators. Ramallah looked
as if it had been smacked and battered into submission. We
shuffled through this gutter of a town going about our daily
lives, managing as best we could, averting our eyes so as not to

see. How else could we survive in this grime and gloom when we had been used to better conditions?

I remember walking in the crowded centre at that time and accidentally brushing against another pedestrian, a middle-aged man. The impact was so light that I did not think an apology was necessary. And yet I found the man turning round and apologising to me profusely, even though it was my fault. It was as though by touching him I had awakened him from some sort of deep reverie; as though he had been so taken up in his own world that the slightest collision had awakened him from a stupor. By apologising he was trying to avoid any sort of trouble and quickly return to his previous state. That was how the old behaved in the stifling confines of our ghetto during the tail end of the Intifada. In the absence of police to enforce law and order, behaving with excessive cordiality seemed to have become a common strategy for survival. Despite the pressures of life in a confined space without physical outlets, walking in the streets one did not encounter many scuffles.

In those last confusing days of the first Intifada, Almaz, the widow of the owner of a haberdashery shop who at seventy-five still thought of herself as a young woman, wore pink dresses and full make-up as she tried to keep up her deceased husband's Nouveautés, the name given to many stores. She lived next to my uncle's house and would come to visit and boast, 'Today I made two shekels.' Once during a snowstorm I offered to drive her home. She got into the car and I asked her to give me directions, but she couldn't. She became very confused. It was a long time before I managed to get her safely to her house. Labibeh, my uncle's wife, visited Almaz just before she died; in fact she was the last person to see her alive. Almaz was in her shabby clothes and it made Labibeh feel sad, so she asked her to put on a fancy robe from when she was young, maybe from her Jaffa days. Almaz did and it was the same robe she was wearing when she was found dead after the balcony of her flat collapsed.

Among the enduring mysteries was the death of the Es Saati Al Almani (the German watchmaker), whose shop was on Main Street next to Almaz's. His was a small shop full of clocks everywhere one looked. As a child I had been there with my mother when she needed to repair her wristwatch. The shop was dark and quiet except for the ticking of the large number of different-sized clocks. Two grandfather clocks stood on either side of the counter behind which Es Saati Al Almani stood. No one called him by any other name; I doubt if anyone knew what his real name was. He spoke little and when he did it was in a heavily accented Arabic. He would grab the watch angrily, as though about to scold my mother for what she has done to his watch, for all of the watches anyone wore in Ramallah came from him. He then picked up his black monocle and pushed it into the socket of his left eye. He had no neck to speak of: his head seemed attached to his shoulders and he was slightly hunched. He wore his trousers high. They came to the middle of his chest, held up by blue braces, making him look like a large football wrapped with two bands. He would flip open the back of the watch and expose the insides. Craning my neck, I would see a whole world of wheels upon wheels, all circling round. What was this ordered world? What was the world of this strange man who came to our city from God knows where and settled here? Both were equally mysterious.

While he was examining the watch and assessing the damage, we would stand very still, holding our breath, concentrating on the ticking of the numerous clocks. It was then that I got the best opportunity to examine the top of his head. He must have been completely bald except for a lining of hair on the lower borders of his scalp. From the back he had taken a very long strand of hair and rolled it again and again over the top of his head. The curling band of hair on his bald head was like the swirling circles in the inside of the exposed watch. The strand of hair was well oiled and pasted to his skull with a heavy dose of Brylcreem, for it never seemed to come unstuck. Sometimes in my more mischievous moods I would imagine pulling the tip of that cake of hair and get it to unfurl for miles and miles. The very thought would excite me, as though I would be undressing this hump of a man. But of course I never dared put my hand anywhere near the frightful head of Es Saati Al Almani.

Eventually he would lift his head and murmur, 'Hmm', while looking at my mother with the black monocle still dangling from his left eye. He looked positively frightening. Then he would quote his price for the repair.

Who was this man? Dr Shawki Harb, a cardiologist from Ramallah who studied medicine in Germany, once spoke to him in German and found that his German was weak. He later told me that this clockmaker could not be German. Where, then, did he come from? Was it Poland or Ukraine or some other East European country? And how did he end up in Ramallah? No one knew his name. His neighbours called him Abu Maurice, though he never had any children. He had no relatives here, only his Palestinian wife. Could he have been a Nazi or a Nazi sympathiser running away from prosecution? Or was he simply a Polish or Ukrainian Jew who ended up on the wrong side of the border? As far as I know, his wife faithfully kept his secret – if she was privy to it, that is – and no one ever knew anything more about this enigmatic man.

He died near his shop. He was crossing the street to go home for lunch at the Salah building, carrying a small plate with a piece of pastry for desert, when a Vespa (motorcycles were a rarity in Ramallah then) hit him, causing him to fall and the plate with the pastry to fly into the air. He died instantly. Was it an accident or an assassination for crimes he had committed in his former life? The Israeli police, having investigated the incident, did not prosecute the driver. They claimed that the German clockmaker died from the impact caused by his head hitting the kerb. No relative came to his funeral or contacted his wife. His secret, whatever it was, was buried with him.

There were a number of other mysterious people in Ramallah. One of these was the knife sharpener, who was always dressed in green and wore a green leather apron. He called himself Al Hamam Al Akhdar (the green dove). He would go around from house to house and people would bring out any knives that needed sharpening. After he finished he lingered to chat with them and hear their news. He was seen riding in an army jeep with the Israeli army when they entered Ramallah after the 1967 occupation.

Had the Intifada brought us independence from Israel and the creation of a Palestinian state, as we had expected and struggled for, perhaps people would have remembered it differently. But ✓ it hadn't, and that was why so many now dread the possibility of more Intifadas.

I spoke to one such person after going, along with some friends, on a spring walk in the lush verdant plains outside Jenin. When it was over, Penny and I decided to pay a visit to the geography professor at Birzeit University, Kamal Abdulfattah, and have coffee with him. This was when I met his wife for the first time. We spoke of what happened in 1989, during the first Intifada, when Kamal was arrested by the Israeli army and prevented from continuing with the geography trip he was leading, which I happened to have joined. He never forgot how I helped defend him on that occasion. At the mention of the Intifada, his wife, who had been the headmistress of a school in Jenin at the time, said, 'I don't want more Intifadas. The two we have already had have brought us nothing. They caused two generations to lose their education and end up ignorant and unskilled. Our suffering was for nothing. My son was fourteen when the soldiers came to take him. He didn't submit easily. He resisted. We were trying to help him when I saw a little box thrown right into our living room. I didn't understand then what it was. But before long the whole place clouded up with smoke and we couldn't breathe. Meanwhile they had managed to take my son away. Once in their jeep they struck his face with a gun. They split his cheek. But this was nothing. It healed. The more serious damage was to his jaw, which they broke. Now when he eats he makes a cracking noise. His children ask him why he makes such a terrible noise when he eats. He has tried to explain to them, make them understand that he can do nothing about it. But how can they? Crack, crack, crack with every bite he takes. This will be with him to the end of his life. That's the legacy of that useless Intifada.'

During the struggle a number of shops in the centre of town were sealed by the occupation soldiers to punish their owners. Cinema Dunia, close to my office on Main Street, was not one of them; instead, its managers decided to close. After years of being abandoned, its front and the display panel showing what films were showing were turned into space for pedlars of cheap merchandise. Plastic bags and paper flew around and collected on street corners. There was not a single clean wall or shopfront. Layer upon layer of graffiti was scrawled in red, green and black, so that it was often hard to make out what they said. One was a drawing of the former Israeli prime minister Yitzhak Shamir as a mouse. And numbers were scrawled there – that was how the army used to call the collaborators they had recruited. There were also plenty of salutes to various political factions and denunciations of collaborators.

The first thing that the new governor of Ramallah, Mustafa Issa, did after the Palestinian Authority took control of the town was to sandblast all the walls and repaint shopfronts in the town centre, removing the graffiti and posters stuck there, an accumulation from the many years of struggle. Indeed, it was his way of asserting that now the PLO was home, the struggle had come to an end. He also proceeded to restore the Manara roundabout, installing four large lions, which was all he could fit there. One of these lions, imported from China, was wearing a watch. It is not clear why, perhaps a sign of the weird times we are living through. He also tried to impose uniform colours for all shopfronts and have barber shops close on Mondays, but this he could not enforce. The newly appointed Palestinian governor of Ramallah was an old-time resident of the city who had joined the resistance outside and returned with the PLO after the Oslo Accords. He was clearly nostalgic for the way things had been when he was growing up in the city and wanted everything to return to how he remembered it.

Next the new Palestinian Authority made an effort to regulate traffic. During the period of Israeli control no traffic lights were allowed because of what the Israelis said were security reasons, and for the safety of their soldiers and settlers, who would not feel safe having to stop at traffic lights in the middle of the Palestinian city. I thought it was admirable how quickly the residents began to comply with the new traffic regulations and how order was returning to the civilian life of the city. Local policemen began to patrol the streets. Most famous was one well-trained wiry young man, impeccably groomed, who directed traffic with strict gestures. Most other policemen, with their ill-fitting uniforms and new unpractised roles, were as ungainly as he was balletic. He seemed like the harbinger of a new, more hopeful future. However, the police did not yet have enforcement powers because the courts were still in disarray and whether or not their orders were followed depended on the mood and social standing of the offender.

Ramallah was transformed by the return of the PLO cadre from Tunis. With the absence of the Israeli army on the streets, nightlife returned. The presence of Israeli soldiers in our midst had meant that, with the first waning of the light, the streets emptied and no one ventured outside. At night the city became a ghost town, free for the Israeli soldiers to carry out their night raids and pull people from their homes to paint over graffiti scribbled on walls and remove stone barricades placed by the activists. I too was woken up at night and made to do this, after which I could not go to bed without wondering whether this was going to be another night when I would be woken up by a knock on the door. The departure of the Israeli army made it safer and less stressful to go out at night. We no longer had to brace ourselves for the prospect of being stopped by the young soldiers, who would amuse themselves at our expense.

The economy was revitalised, mainly by EU and US donors' money and investments encouraged and often sponsored by the World Bank and other governments who were interested in making the Oslo deal work. But the benefit was restricted only to some. Ramallah became the centre of the Palestinian Authority and this attracted more internal migrants. My law office represented some of the new investors. This meant that I needed to return to dressing up in a suit and tie and going to meetings. I once hailed a taxi to take me to one such meeting. It was warm and I was wearing a new white shirt with a starched collar. Before getting into the taxi, I removed my jacket and put on the seat belt, as the new short-lived regulations required. Immediately after I did this I noticed that my white shirt was stained by a band of dirt across the front, like a sash. It was grime from the long years of the Intifada when seat belts were not in use and there was much soot in the air from the burning of tyres.

The city and its inhabitants were trying to catch up with the world after years of dormancy and restrictions on development that the occupation had imposed. From a sleepy town, the place became vital and active again as we tried to lick our wounds and catch up with the progress we had missed. Ramallah's residents were learning quickly to enjoy nightlife, going out on the streets at night and visiting the restaurants, cafés and theatres that were mushrooming everywhere. Many Palestinians returning with the PLO were now urbanised, having lived in Beirut and Tunis, and were used to such nightlife. Their presence in Ramallah made a difference. The new eateries and nightclubs encouraged young Israelis, curious about the Ramallah they had heard of from the news but had not seen, to come and spend evenings there. The local police, even though generally still lame, also gave a greater sense of security than had existed before. Drinking and dancing parties resumed.

With the new mood and increase in consumerism the Christmas season, which had always been celebrated in Ramallah, now became a highly commercial extravaganza, with many shops employing young men to wear Santa outfits and roam the streets, shaking their little bells to encourage potential shoppers. One foreign woman got into the spirit of Christmas and, when approached by Papa Noël, greeted him with an enthusiastic, 'Merry Christmas,' to which his immediate response was, 'Fuck you.'

Such was the mixture of reactions to attempts at regulating the life of the city and moving it forward. The town was like an adolescent learning to flex his muscles, flailing his strong arms and causing random damage all around. Some welcomed these changes and began to make up for lost time and lost opportunities for making money and enjoying themselves, while others were disaffected and decided to emigrate. To them these changes were just a façade that amounted to a repackaging of the old oppression and occupation without ending it.

In the wake of the accelerated development in my city, a number of historical buildings fell victim to the greed of developers. One of these was the attractive building of Cinema Dunia, which was demolished, only to be replaced by a bulky complex totally out of proportion with its surroundings, called Dunia Mall. The cinema was where the Jaffa refugees in Ramallah had met in the summer of 1948, when my father and others proposed that they return to Jaffa. 'The road is open,' they said. 'Why should we not go back?' It was resolved that they would all do so, en masse. The next day, before this could happen, he and the other leaders who took part in that meeting were taken prisoners by the Jordanian army under Glub Pasha. Now the building where that historic meeting took place has gone and no plaque commemorating the event has been placed there. The post-Nakba generations are not even aware that such an attempt at a return was ever planned, or that it was aborted by the Arab army.

One of Faik's sons, Ayman, works as a taxi driver. Not long ago, I hailed a taxi and he stopped for me. I asked about his father. He told me that Faik was now retired, after having had open-heart surgery.

'My mother,' Ayman said, 'is in her sixties, but if you look at her she looks like a woman of eighty.'

'And Amjad, how is he?' I asked.

'He's been imprisoned eighteen times. He's an important leader in Fatah. Every time he left prison he resumed his activism in the struggle. The last time he was given a lengthy sentence which will end in four years. He's now forty-seven. He's the leader at Nafha prison, where he is now.'

Ayman told me that in 1989, when he was involved in the first Intifada, he was shot in the gut. I realise that not one of Faik's sons has escaped being killed, injured or imprisoned. And he took them out of the camp in order to keep them away from politics.

When I expressed sorrow at the death of his brother Muhamad, Ayman said, 'It's everyone's wish to be martyred.' Then he added, 'This was his fate. He died fighting.'

Neither Ayman nor his parents can visit Amjad in prison because the brothers have convictions and the parents are the parents of activists. For the hundreds of young men who have been in Israeli prisons, the prison becomes like a collective where men live together at close quarters, cook and eat together. Some, like Ayman, emulate this at their place of work. The taxi office where he works has a kitchen. The drivers take turns cooking and cleaning and every day they all eat lunch together, like one large family.

Even after I left him, Ayman's words about fate and martyrdom kept going round in my head and I thought that surely this was one way of coming to terms with a tragic death.

It was young activists like Ayman and Muhamad who started the second disastrous armed Intifada. The first had been a true war of liberation, a secular revolt, an opening to something new, an opportunity to create a different kind of society; and for me personally, it was my first experience of collective struggle. But then Hamas entered the political arena. At first Israel did nothing: they did not list it as a prohibited organisation and did not stop it from receiving funds from outside. Then, in 1992, soon after the peace negotiations began, they deported a large number of its members to south Lebanon, where they received training in military warfare from the Lebanese Hezbollah. For a long time Israel was desperate to split the nationalist movement in Palestine. They were loath to recognise the PLO before it acquired a Palestinian rival. Now the leadership is split, with Hamas running Gaza and Fatah the West Bank. At last Israel has succeeded, like every colonizer, to divide and rule.

Even our vocabulary has changed. No one can now call death by its name if it occurs in the course of struggle. The other day I went to Kashou's hardware shop to get a nozzle for the garden hose. I noticed that the proprietor's son was just opening up the iron shutters, as the other shop owners were doing. I asked why the closure and he said in his slow, calm matter-of-fact voice, 'Someone died. He's not from Ramallah but from the outskirts and they asked us to close from ten to eleven.' As the father was speaking I heard his son muttering '*istashhad*' (he was martyred) almost with a desperate groan, as if to say, how many times must I remind you to use the right words: *istashhad*, not *itwafa* (he was martyred, not died).

I was reminded of this change in the language in how we refer to death when I heard Samia Halaby, the famous Palestinian artist, talking about her drawings of the massacre of Kafr Qasim, which took place on 29 October 1956 in Israel. She was speaking in Arabic about her research, investigations and work on the massacre. Her choice of words and her manner were those of an older time, a time that has passed and been fundamentally changed. She called death by its name, dying by its name, and said that when the soldiers *takhu* (shot) the Palestinians they *matu* (died). She did not say *istashhadu*, or call death *shahada* or the dead *shaheed*. Her vocabulary alerted me to how death has been camouflaged and altered to become something else, something more palatable, not final but a noble elevated passage to heaven, in order to help those who lose loved ones endure their loss. Yet however it is referred to, even Ayman knows deep down that death is the final destination.

Now, on the fiftieth anniversary of the occupation, I am again walking up Irsal Street to the Muqata'a, and thinking how this occupation has accompanied me most of my life. It has walked with me like a shadow, stalking me, sometimes posing a challenge but more often a threat. At times I have tried doggedly to shake it off, live as though it were not there, but it always proved stronger and reasserted its presence. And so I've come to accept that it is my karma to live under it. When I was young I rebelled against my fate and tried to escape its clutches, but it proved too tenacious. Even when I travelled it came along and refused to leave me alone. And now as I stroll through the Ramallah streets I come across so many reminders that bring everything back. There were times when we hoped that we were getting rid of the occupation and I worked and lived for that moment. But it dissipated twenty-four years ago with the first Oslo Accord, and since then I've lived without hope, constantly trying to adjust to life and accept that it will only go from bad to worse as the occupation becomes more entrenched, grabbing more of our land and tightening the noose around our necks.

The lines from Auden's poem 'Spain' about the Spanish Civil War come to mind:

We are left alone with our day, and the time is short, and
History to the defeated
May say Alas but cannot help or pardon.

Eleven

Near the start of Irsal Street, where one of the tall new buildings now stands, there used to be a house with a green glass balcony and a garden that belonged to a Russian, Dr George Rudenko. He had escaped the civil war in Ukraine and made his way to Palestine, working in a hospital in Jaffa during the British Mandate. There he married a Palestinian nurse and was forced to leave in 1948, ending up in Ramallah. He had a tall and imposing figure and often wore a wide-brimmed black hat. He was a friend of my father's and we often visited him in Irsal Street. A passionate hunter, he kept white plastic ducks on the table in his living room that he used as decoys when hunting. As a child I enjoyed squeezing those ducks.

Irsal Street used to be called Lovers' Street. It was lined with old pine trees. From there one could look northwest at the hills and see spectacular panoramic sunsets. A refreshing cool breeze always blew on this elevated part of Ramallah. Not any more. Now the views have been blocked by the tall buildings that hug the street and so too has the wind.

The recitation from the Quran that precedes the afternoon

call to prayer starts to come through amplifiers placed on the tall Natsheh building in the centre of town, interrupting this reverie. Coming towards me I see four Palestinian policemen with black masks covering their faces up to their eyes, plastic shields held against their chests, and kneepads. Carrying batons and guns, they are walking down the street to attract attention: a demonstration of strength by the Palestinian security services. The weather is too warm for such attire. The unfortunate young men must be boiling, I think. They are roaming around to make sure that on this fiftieth anniversary of the Israeli occupation everyone toes the line. What did it take to train these young men to shift their view of the enemy, from the occupier to any Palestinian who dares challenge the Palestinian Authority and those in control of our reduced territory?

The young here have no notion of what the city was like before the massive developments that have taken place over the past two decades. They relish its Americanisation and many come from the nearby villages to eat out at the KFC and Pizza Hut across the street from where I stand. These two places are always crowded. Sometimes I wonder where I am. This does not feel like the Ramallah I knew.

The stubbornly dull and sleepy provincial town I grew up in has developed into a flourishing city, with many places of entertainment and a rich cultural life. The city's population went through a tremendous transformation after most of its original inhabitants left. Now, like most other cities around the world, it has a mixed population. With all my nostalgia for the way things were, life in modern Ramallah is much more exciting and culturally diverse than was ever the case in the past. I might sometimes feel like a stranger here and despondent about the future, yet the young have many more opportunities than my generation did at their age, naïve and unconnected as we were to the rest of the world. They will forge ahead; they might even be more successful than we were in achieving liberation.

Halfway along Irsal Street are the newly constructed headquarters of the President of the Palestinian Authority, built on the site of the demolished Tegart building, or Muqata'a, as we now call it. The Tegart was one of some fifty such structures built by the British in 1938 in various parts of Palestine. They were established by Sir Charles Tegart, a former commissioner of police in Calcutta, who was sent to Palestine as a counterterrorism expert in the midst of the 1936 Palestinian popular revolt against Mandate rule. In 2002, when the compound served as Yasser Arafat's headquarters, it was bombed by the Israeli army after the reinvasion of Ramallah. Two years later it remained unrepaired. I can still remember how it looked on a misty winter's morning in 2004 when I went to check whether any work had been done there. I could see the ruins behind a milky-white foreground. The pine trees were still standing, as was the façade of what had once served as the Israeli Civil Administration, where one went for permits and, when summoned, for interrogation. By the gate was a sign pointing to a complaints box which must have been placed there by a cynical Israeli soldier as a sick joke. Not surprisingly, the box was always empty. The only possible complaint that any of us wanted to make was against the very existence of the occupation. Remarkably, also still standing were the four steps leading up to the small balcony of the stone building next to the cement Tegart structure. These must have been built later than the rest. Beyond, through the windows of the façade, one could see piles of earth, demolished cement structures, twisted iron and aluminium. Columns that had been severed from the bottom hung from the crumpled, collapsed roof over the courtyard like giant icicles. A few tattered Palestinian flags fluttered forlornly here and there over the ruins. Close to the street on the southwestern side of the compound were the demolished remains of the cubicles which had once served as toilets for those waiting to visit prisoners. They formed a strange sight, with their exposed fronts revealing the porcelain of the toilets, creating a strange glossy seam in the ruins.

Memories come back of an earlier visit, just after the Israeli army withdrew from Ramallah in January 1995. I remember walking into the liberated compound, into the rooms where prisoners were kept, and choking in the stiflingly tiny cells where they were held in solitary confinement for weeks on end, reading the graffiti that, in their desperation, they had scribbled on the walls and the marks they had made to keep track of time. These cells are now empty. There was a prison here and then there was no prison. Yet the prison is all around us.

During my visit I found that the Tegart where Arafat had lived and worked remained in its decrepit state long after he died, the sole physical reminder of what the city had endured two years earlier. This was not without design. It served to highlight the endurance of our leader. There, in the midst of the ruins, the man of symbols lived as the most potent symbol of steadfastness, far superior to any we could ever claim. How could we possibly voice any grievance against his style of leadership or the consequences of his decisions or the fact that little remained of Palestine except symbols, when he had endured such hardship on our behalf? I remember thinking that the luxury of moving forward and consigning the horrors of the past to a building that is turned into a museum was not ours.

Perhaps it cannot be, not until the occupation ends. The suffering we used to endure at the Tegart has only been transferred to what is now the Civil Administration, with its headquarters at the former Jordanian military hospital, which is now Beit El. Yet, as I discovered recently, some of my friends had remained unaware that the Israeli Civil Administration, which controlled so many aspects of Palestinian life, had not been abolished but merely transferred from the Tegart to Beit El. A few nights ago I went to dinner at our neighbour Randa's house and heard the reactions to the ordeal suffered by Maha, another friend, which she described to us.

maha's narrative ↓

'I had that stupid idea that I would save my son, Ramiz, the humiliation of leaving Palestine via the Israeli-controlled Allenby Bridge into Jordan and take him out through the airport. So yesterday morning I decided to try and obtain a permit. I asked where you got these permits and was directed to the Civil Administration,' said Maha, who looked exhausted by what she had been through.

'It still exists? I thought it went with Oslo,' Muneer said.

'What do you mean "went"? Where have you been living?'

'Seriously, I thought it was done away with. Didn't it used to be at the Muqata'a?'

'That was a long time ago. Now it is at the edge of the settlement of Beit El. I can't believe you're so innocent. You mean you've never had the pleasure of going there?'

'I haven't left Ramallah for three years.'

'Well, lucky you.'

'I haven't left for five,' Hani declared.

'But you will soon,' Randa said. 'Aren't you travelling with Maha and Ramiz?'

'No, I can't. They're going alone. You see, a few years ago I got a green card. But I was unable to travel to the States. It's now five years since I've been there so the card has lost its validity. And I can't get a US visa because I have a green card. So I'm stuck. But I don't really want to travel.'

There was something odd about the way that Hani was revealing his situation to us. It was as though he was revelling in his desperate predicament. He didn't want our sympathy, that was clear. Why, then, was he telling us all this? Perhaps because he wanted to justify leaving his wife, Maha, alone to suffer the humiliation of waiting outside the door of the most dreaded office in the West Bank. Beneath the quiet exterior was an angry, frustrated man.

'So, let me enlighten you. Just in case, God forbid, you decide to travel. You must first drive in the direction of Beit El. But you can't drive all the way. The road is blocked. I had to park by the side of the road and walk on the Ramallah–Nablus highway, which is also closed, until I got to the earth mound. I climbed this. Good thing I was wearing my old shoes. Once over this new feature of our landscape, I got to the empty car park into which West Bank cars are not allowed. And there I saw the shacks with the corrugated-iron roofs topped with sandbags and barbed wire, and an empty watchtower, the famous Civil Administration. There it was: four windows with faded signs in Hebrew and Arabic indicating where the different sorts of permits can be applied for. A large crowd of people of all ages had gathered at the windows. At the head of the line I saw the ubiquitous burly young man who immediately makes himself useful. In this case he was acting as interpreter from Arabic to Hebrew. He was also collecting all the permit applications and pushing them through the small openings in the windows, protected by iron bars, so that the soldier-clerks who were invisible to the rest of us could begin to process them. I asked someone close by whether anyone had confirmed that there were people inside. No one knew. Still the efforts to deliver the permit applications continued until the rumour came at ten o'clock that our applications had been processed and the responses were ready. Everyone sighed with relief.

'It seemed just a matter of time before we would hear back from the invisible soldiers. There was a perceptible reduction in tension. We all just had to wait. For how long, I did not know. I found myself a ledge to sit on and began sweating under the hot sun. There wasn't any sort of shelter. I regretted not bringing a hat and for the first time in my life envied those women wearing the hijab.'

'There were other women there as well?' Muneer asked.

'Certainly. Why, did you assume I was the only woman? In fact there was an almost exact gender balance. I bought myself a cold drink, sat down and waited. Soon I regretted drinking. There were toilets around but they were filthy, the worst I have yet seen. The swarms of flies, which, alas, had access to both the toilets and us, were beyond belief. I bet the soldiers' windows had screens.'

Muneer asked, 'What happened next?'

'Not much. I was there from nine until eleven thirty, when we heard the announcement that the soldiers were going for their lunch break and would reopen the windows at one o'clock sharp. Lots of comments could now be heard about the kind of food awaiting the soldiers and wishes for their good digestion floated about. And then we waited. One o'clock came and went and nothing happened. No sign of life could be detected behind the barred windows. This silence continued until two o'clock, when we heard a rustle from the other side of the window through which my application for the two permits had been slipped. A huge crowd of hopefuls now pushed ahead waving their identity cards, waiting for their names to be called. But nothing happened. This turned out to be a false alarm. The rustle had not been of any consequence. For all we knew, it could have been the wind or the fan going on for some odd reason inside the shack, or a careless soldier brushing against the curtain on his way in or out. At this point a young man strategically situated at the window told me that he had just seen my papers with the new pile to be submitted when the window reopened after lunch. And all this time I was under the false belief that my papers had been submitted with the ten o'clock batch.

'Then, at two forty-five, the curtain was pulled aside. Within fifteen minutes the soldier received the new pile of applications and the applicants remarked triumphantly that now they have been submitted it would only be a short wait for the results. At three o'clock names were called out, but only from the morning batch. With all the commotion and noise it was impossible to hear the names called in a faint voice from behind the window with the iron bars by a soldier who did not wish to expend much energy in this exercise that he cared nothing about. So it fell to our interpreter of the morning to save the day by shouting out the names as he heard them from the invisible soldier. The most common word uttered after most of the names was *marfood* [refused]. But the interesting thing was that with every cry of *marfood* everyone clapped, rather cheerfully, I thought. This lightened up the atmosphere as we watched the subject of the rejection tread away amid consolations offered by the rest of the crowd. Most of those who did not get a straight-out *marfood* got a provisional rejection. They were told to support their applications with a doctor's report, employer's testimony and the like, and to come back with this documentation next day. For these the crowd did not cheer.

'By four it was clear that my papers had indeed gone with the afternoon batch. There was a quick succession of *marfood*s and then silence. I was reassured by a young man who seemed to be in the know that they call out the rejectees' names first. The fact that I had not been called was a good omen. At four fifty I heard my name being called. But to get to the window through the crowd was no easy matter. Some of the men had climbed on top of the railings in order to have a better view of the proceedings behind the iron bars. But as soon as I began to move forward the gallant crowd allowed the right amount of space for a woman to approach the window. Once there I heard the soldier barking out something in Hebrew. What on earth was he saying? I tried English with him but to no avail. By this time a new interpreter had positioned himself where the first had been. He must have already left with his *marfood*. The interpreter made it clear to me that I was among the *marfood* crowd and I too got cheered when the word was heard down the line. Seven hours of agony, all wasted. Leaving the shack, I saw a foreign woman driving in confidently where no West Bank cars were allowed. The soldier yelled at her to move the car, but she had enough self-confidence and connections to refuse. I had the sense that she was there to get airport permits for Palestinians invited abroad by her organisation or government. They needed little intercession from the army, so they could depart through the airport and not suffer the indignities of the route through Jordan.

'At this point I found myself boiling with rage. I leapt at her car and began screaming at her. "You are here to get permits for your staff?" I asked.

'"Yes," she responded proudly.

'"You should be ashamed of yourself," I said.

'"Why?" she asked, surprised. "I'm not responsible for the occupation."

'By now I was screaming. I pointed out that I wished the hundreds of people over there had this same privilege. But she had had enough of my outburst and was trying to escape. I wouldn't let up, though.

'I still don't understand what brought about my outburst,' Maha went on to say. 'It was so unlike me to blow up like that and let all my anger and frustration out on this woman.'

'You were right to give her a piece of your mind,' said Muneer.

'Maybe she was using her privilege, but her response was

correct. She was not responsible for the occupation and I had no right to blow up. You should have seen me. I was screaming. She tried to get away from me but I wouldn't let her. I, the quiet, usually polite Maha, was holding this woman hostage and wouldn't let her go until I had poured out all the rage that had been building up from the heat, the injustice, the hopelessness of our situation and the clouds of dust that flew up at us every time one of her kind drove their car nearby, covering us with muck as though to emphasise our inferior status. My parting words to her were that she should examine her conscience and see if she was not perpetuating our agony.'

'We all lose our patience with the situation at some time and let everything out,' our gentle hostess told Maha. 'Don't let it bother you.'

The new headquarters of the Palestinian Authority which I am now passing, built next to the old Muqata'a, are a sharp contrast to those where Yasser Arafat worked. Mahmoud Abbas, the present head of the Authority, operates out of headquarters built with clean, well-chiselled white limestone fronted by well-trimmed grass, suggesting a sombre, organised and orderly organisation, not one leading a struggle for independence from the occupier. As I pass this gleaming structure, I wonder whether the point of removing all remnants of the old Muqata'a was to make us forget the travails of the past and believe that a new, post-struggle era has begun. As a result of the levelling of the old Tegart, there is no place where the young can experience what our generation went through and endured. My nephew Aziz and his contemporaries can no longer visit the window in the small porch of what was called the Civil Administration, behind which we crammed day in, day out, waiting for one or another of the many permits needed for all sorts of activities, whether travel, driving or getting a telephone line;

or see for themselves in the next part of the building the tiny cells where the prisoners were held in solitary confinement, sometimes for weeks and months; or see the torture chambers where the heroic fighters of my generation suffered, read what they scribbled on the walls and see at first-hand the conditions of their incarceration. Likewise the Ottoman building which served as the Ramallah police station, where so many suffered, was also destroyed by a large bomb dropped by an Israeli helicopter gunship. It is as though the Israeli authorities and the Palestinian officials have worked together to obliterate these sites of great suffering, stopping the young from experiencing what it was like under full Israeli rule.

I decide to visit the Arafat Museum and Mausoleum, which have been built on the ruin of the old Tegart. A gleaming white walkway led to Arafat's grave. There were pink and red sweet williams and a well-maintained lawn. The landscaping was good, with large boulders to break the level ground. A tower is topped with a gadget that is supposed to send a ray of light towards Jerusalem, the city that he failed to liberate. Perhaps it is meant to symbolise the unrealised hope of reaching it some day. The museum, which is next to the mausoleum, is well designed but tells the Palestinian story through a selective presentation of material, remarkable for what is left out. The story is told entirely from the point of view of the Palestine Liberation Organisation. Palestinian history is presented as beginning with the British Mandate, as though we had no history prior to that. Totally missing is any representation of the *sumoud* (steadfastness) of those of us living under occupation for half a century or the solidarity and struggle of Palestinians living in Israel. The curator (who, I'm told, is Egyptian) could have easily chosen to highlight the life story of one of the heroic symbols of *sumoud*, such as Sabri Ghraib, who struggled from 1979 until his death in 2012 against the Jewish settlement of

Givon Hadasha, established on his land and that of his village. Despite years of harassment and assiduous efforts to evict him from his house, he managed to hold on to some of his land and continued to live in his house, which the settlement eventually encircled. Or Muhammad Abdeh, who has held on to his house in Gush Etzion. Or Sa'deah Al Bakri, who managed for years to live in her house next to the settlement of Kiryat Arba, despite continuous attacks by the settlers on her, her children and their house. Surely these and many more heroes of *sumoud* deserve recognition.

The main story is the doomed armed struggle. And yet the presentation is neither self-congratulatory nor valorous. So much so that the couple behind me, especially the woman, kept repeating, '*Hasrah alena wain kuna u wain surna*' ('For pity's sake! Look where we were, and where we are now').

There are photographs of numerous leaders assassinated by Israel over the many years of struggle. The negotiations leading to the signing of the Oslo Accords on the White House lawn are presented as a victory for the Palestinians, with endless photographs of Arafat's travels to the capitals of the world, where he was met as a head of state. The fact that this encouraged countries like India, which had refused to have any relations with Israel until Oslo, is not mentioned.

The story narrated by the museum ends on the ground level at Arafat's 'bunker', the only section of the Tegart that has been preserved, where he was trapped during the six-month siege of the Muqata'a that began on 29 March 2002. Earlier we had been shown footage of the Israeli bulldozers demolishing parts of the Tegart after its bombardment. It is as though we, in the image of Arafat, remain hostages to Israeli intransigence and aggression, which neither wane nor show any sign of ending.

Seeing the museum and how it portrays the struggle without giving due credit to the *sumoud* of those living in the occupied territories dampened my spirits. There is absolutely no recognition here of past mistakes. But then a national museum is hardly the place for that. It is generally the case that when a people's struggle is over, one group represents how it was won. But in our case the struggle is neither over nor won, and what keeps it going is nothing other than our *sumoud*.

There is no doubt that Arafat's endurance of the bombardment in those last six months of his life was heroic. He presents an apt symbol for Palestinians under threat. But what is one to make of this symbol? Had the struggle succeeded, it would have been right to showcase it. But it didn't. It is ongoing. What, then, is the point of overshadowing the ongoing endurance of the rest of the population, who are still suffering? Or is Arafat's story meant to produce some form of catharsis in a long-lasting tragedy?

His tragedy (or rather ours) – his legacy – is that he failed to leave behind a democratic system, a process by which the top man seeks and receives counsel and decisions are taken collectively. The Palestinian Authority which he left behind pays no heed to advisers who could help it build a more effective strategy in the face of the massive Israeli challenges. And look where we have got to: we are totally subservient, defeated and dominated by Israel in every way. The revisionist history of the Palestinian struggle has yet to be written. Hopefully, some day it will be represented in a more balanced national museum. Meanwhile in the streets of Ramallah I saw a banner on which was written: 'If they should ask you which country you come from answer them: I come from a country whose history is Yasser Arafat.'

My first impression upon leaving the well-groomed gardens of the museum and returning to Irsal Street is that the city is no longer involved in a collective struggle against the occupation. Each of us is on our own. This is evident in the way people are

driving. I can see no posters of *shuhada* (martyrs) on the walls –
they are removed as soon as they appear. The only posters are
for banks, advertising 'How to Win a Million'.

The city has aged and changed almost beyond recognition
from the time I was growing up. In these past fifty years it has
suffered two major invasions, in 1967 and 2002. It survived both
and flourished and is now claimed by the young. They are more
savvy and connected to the rest of the world than my generation ever was. This provides new opportunities for economic
development and struggle. In the old days at Al Haq we tried to
wage campaigns against widespread Israeli human rights violations, but without internet, mail or uncensored international
phone lines our options were few. We understood what was
happening but couldn't do much to stop it. Now they can and
have waged worldwide campaigns like BDS (Boycott, Divest-
ment and Sanctions) that might end up deterring Israel, as
happened in South Africa. The Arafat Museum, built on the
ruins of the Tegart, represents the past. It is the story of one
aspect of our struggle leading to no heroic end, no climax. That
phase of the struggle is over. Yet by no means is the struggle
itself over. The words of Matthew Arnold in 'Dover Beach'
come to mind:

> And we are here as on a darkling plain
> Swept with confused alarms of struggle and flight,
> Where ignorant armies clash by night.

A few months ago I went to the new cemetery for the burial of a
friend's mother. This cemetery is located on high ground at the
very edge of town, not far from the wall separating Ramallah
from the nearby Jewish settlement of Givat Ze'ev. From
there the wall is visible, as is the separation of the city from
its surroundings. It was a lengthy struggle to get permission

from the Israelis to build it there. Israel even fears the dead. So crowded was the old cemetery that father used to say, 'The way things are going we'll not find a spot to be buried.'

Standing there and looking at the settlement made me think of how all the exits from the city have been closed. The Beitunia exit from Jaffa Street is blocked by the Ofer prison and army camp. Only commercial traffic, merchandise brought from Israel for sale in Ramallah, is allowed through. The exit through Masyoun is also blocked at Jeeb and Bir Nabala, with a terrible maze of walls and tunnels for Palestinians driving below the settler road connecting Jerusalem and the settlements to the coastal cities. And so is the exit to Jerusalem at Kalandia. Ramallah has become like a city-state, its links to the rest of the West Bank severed by checkpoints. No wonder it acts like a bubble, unconcerned with or inattentive to what is happening to those living in the countryside around it, or to the suffering of those living in the Gaza Strip.

It was my first visit to this new cemetery. I was surprised that there was a sign saying 'Christian cemetery'. I thought this strange but later realised that just above was another sign for another part of the cemetery saying 'Muslim cemetery'. So the co-religionists are buried side by side; they live and die together. But my resting place will not be here. It will be in the old cemetery, along with my family, fresh bones on top of charcoal bones. The graves of my grandparents and my parents are there. It is true that I never visit my father's grave, but then I never believe this is where he is, or my mother. In death I celebrate them in my own way, as I always insisted on my own way of relating to them in life. Even though my grandfather Salim died in Beirut, he had asked to be buried in Ramallah. Continuity? Perhaps. With father there remains much that is unsaid, incomplete, unrealised. A relationship which during his life I managed badly. My visit today to our old houses has

helped ease some of the burden of the guilt and regret that I
have long harboured.

I have now walked to the end of Irsal. At one corner, the road
going east leads to the boulevard that dignitaries visiting the
Palestinian Authority drive along after crossing the Israeli
checkpoint called DCO, in reference to the District Coordi-
nation Office there. Another of the Ramallah exits which is
blocked. The government spent a lot of money to make the
road leading into the city from that checkpoint as impressive as
possible, following the practice of most impoverished countries
in making every effort to keep out of sight any evidence of
poverty from the main artery leading from the airport to the
posh hotels where they stay. After Oslo we had high hopes that
Palestine would have an airport of its own. The DCO is all we
got. When dignitaries come to visit our president in Ramallah,
Palestinian soldiers can be seen with their armoured cars parked
at the corner leading to the checkpoint, unable to venture any
further, as though they are waiting at a proper border of their
state, when all it is is a border that isn't a border. The DCO
separates Palestinian territory from other Palestinian territory
within the West Bank. When the dignitaries arrive these soldiers
accompany them in an impressive parade, while other foot
soldiers line the streets of Ramallah all the way to their hotel.

To my left as I face the road leading downhill to Birzeit,
north of Ramallah, is a grand building in the shape of a ship,
hence its name, Al Safineh. It is narrow in front and tilted up
like a bow, with round windows on the side and a chimney on
top flying the national flag. In this 'ship' there is a Caribbean
restaurant flying the Jolly Roger with its skull and crossbones.
The front is directed towards the horizon and the Mediterranean Sea as though ready to sail. It made me think of T. S.
Eliot's 'Gerontion': 'Signs are taken for wonders. "We would

see a sign!"' This strange structure confirms my impression of Ramallah as a city of illusions inhabited by aspirants, poised to take off but prevented by the forces of circumstance and misfortune. As I look at this building the conversation with the taxi driver who drove me home the other day came to mind.

'There are no horizons,' he told me. 'Life here is beginning to feel more like life in a prison. I drive around all day in my car yet feel so confined, as though I am going in circles, in a world that keeps on shrinking. I yearn to drive long distances, use the fourth and fifth gears of my car for a change, to speed along a highway that stretches to eternity with empty space on both sides and not a single human being in sight. Is this asking too much? But I know that the confinement is only going to get worse. Soon the wall around Ramallah will be completed and we will have to enter and leave through a gate, same as in a prison.'

'Why, then, do you stay?' I asked provocatively.

He answered in a serious manner, indicating that he had given much thought to the matter. He said, 'I have considered my situation very carefully and decided I am much better off leaving. This is no life. But where can I go? There is no country that will accept me. This is the only reason I stay.'

At the ship I turn back. When I reach the crossroads near the new Muqata'a, I turn right and walk down Ayn Musbah Street, which circles the centre of the city, passing by the old spring from which the people in this part of Ramallah used to fetch water before there was running water. When I pass Dar Sa'a in the old city, I remember the exhibition, entitled *Pattern Recognition*, that I had visited there last year. The new Ramallah has an impressive output of culture and art, which had been rare in the old Ramallah I grew up in. One video stood out. It was called *Yamm* (Hebrew for sea) and was by Ruba Salameh, who

was born in Nazareth in 1985. It showed people waiting for a minibus with traffic passing by against a poster of the Gaza Sea, animated with an insertion of film fragments shot from the beach at Tantoura in Israel. It was accompanied by the following text: 'Shown in Ramallah, the work ties together the fragmentary nature of Palestinian geography: Gaza, the West Bank, Jerusalem and the territory of 1948. For many Palestinians, travelling the route of this very map has become an impossibility.'

As twilight descends, filled with hope and misgivings, I now walk home with hurried steps.

Twelve

The streets are clogged with traffic as people rush back home before the evening call to prayer that indicates the end of the day's fast. Some are just cruising around, exhibiting their new cars bought with loans from the bank, playing loud music. Such a cacophony. There is too much light to be able to see the stars. I try to remember how it used to be when I walked home with my grandmother from the Grand Hotel. Then there were few street lights, many broken by bored children throwing stones, competing over who had the better aim. The stars would be visible and there would be almost total silence, with only the occasional car passing. As we walked home together I could hear our footsteps and the click-click-click of *Tata's* wooden cane on the paving stones.

'Muffle up. We don't want your tummy to get cold,' she would say as we struggled against the wind from the distant Mediterranean coast that always hit us as soon as we turned the corner from Main Street to Ahlia Street.

I walk faster, trying to make it home before dark, thinking how the city I grew up in has remained with me. I am able to see both the old and the new, how it was and how it has become. When I was younger I was unable to see myself the way people saw me. I looked at the older people around me and felt dismayed at how they had aged. Now that I have neither 'youth nor age', I feel more tolerant and loving. I only hope that the time will come for me, as it did for poet Derek Walcott:

> when, with elation
> you will greet yourself arriving
> at your own door, in your own mirror
> and each will smile at the other's welcome.

I used to believe that as I walked among the people of my city I was mysterious, an enigma. I wondered what they made of my often shabby dress and manifestations of rebellion. I don't any more. I think they always knew me, perhaps better than I knew myself. They read me like an open book. My family is known, my lineage, my history, my capabilities and failures – though perhaps not so much through what has meant the most to me, my writing. For the others I was only the lawyer. For many years Al Haq, which has become a well-respected public institution, was associated with my name, but that was mainly for an earlier generation.

And yet even though I have lived all my life in the same small city, I have never felt at ease with the society or truly a part of it. I was always at odds with the tradition, a rebel, even when I yearned to belong. I always was, and will remain, an outsider. This may be why I've continued to be troubled by a recurrent dream of searching for a home.

This feeling of being a stranger was shared by my maternal grandfather, Boulos Shehadeh, the poet, who towards the end of his short life published a poem called 'Despair' in which he wrote:

The time of departure is nigh
who will have tears to shed for me?
I'm but a stranger in these lands who has outstayed his time

As I approach my house, the shadow following me lengthens as the sun begins to set on my city. Thomas Gainsborough, the British portrait and landscape painter, thought that all landscape was light and shadow. I wonder how this applied to writing. With my words I have tried to shed light on my city. As I move closer to home, my own shadow diminishes, so that by the time I arrive it has disappeared altogether. I am struck by the thought that when I'm gone not even my shadow will remain.

Before opening the gate, I look at my house with the soft rosy light of the setting sun striking the limestone walls. The feathery leaves of the jacaranda in the garden hug the walls and shed their shadows over the entrance I am now approaching. Our house is rather grand, I think, and turned inward. I have never looked at it this way before. Now I can see how like me it is. This is how I survived in my society with its inflexibility and constant failures and retreats: by being like the house – walled, stubborn, centred, inward-looking, impregnable, with a mind of my own and my own peculiar ways. I wanted to escape my predicament, find consolation in abstraction and turn suffering into art.

Near the kerb, a short distance from the entrance, I notice the caper plant that I had looked at on my way out this morning. I see that its pods have opened. This bushy plant is growing out of bare rock yet it flourishes, even without water. Its round alternate leaves, thick, hardy and shiny, are mauve in colour. And among them the most beautiful flowers are blooming, composed of delicate pink-white petals and long violet stamens, with a single stigma rising above the stamens, all surrounded by four sepals waving gently in the slight breeze. Such a refreshing sight in these dry hills. No gardener has cultivated this bush. And perhaps, except for the spikes with which the plant protected itself, it might have been pulled up and destroyed. Needing little organic matter to grow and able to withstand high temperatures, this delicate but hardy shrub has established itself in these hills. It is capable of surviving in tough conditions, producing luscious fruit in many different places around the world. I would like to think of myself in those terms.

I am about to open the gate and enter the courtyard that leads to our main door, when I briefly glance back at the hills that can be seen beyond the empty plot between the buildings across the street. They look almost pink as the limestone reflects the setting sun. I want to linger and hold on to this day, another good day in the short time that is left to me.

The dark purple of the bougainvillea is clashing with the setting sun. The plumbago is in full bloom. Neither in the first family house nor at Helen's did I have a garden that did so well. It is only in this house that I managed to create such a satisfying one.

I linger a bit longer outside the gate until the sun has gone and the moon is visible. I can see the solanum with its blue flowers closing for the night. From the house I can hear a Handel opera that Penny is listening to. I decide to wait for the aria to finish before proceeding. I may have missed out on many pleasures because of my physical vulnerability, but I have other satisfactions. A fragment of Wordsworth's 'Tintern Abbey' comes to me:

> … wild ecstasies shall be matured
> Into a sober pleasure; when thy mind
> Shall be a mansion for all lovely forms,
> Thy memory be as a dwelling-place
> For all sweet sounds and harmonies …

The gate clicks shut behind me. I recall doing the same before the 2002 Israeli invasion of Ramallah. Then I was coming back home with supplies from the market. Once inside my house, I fantasised that I would be safe, that it could not happen to me. I had been going on with my life, trying to remain out of sight, keeping to myself, stirring as few ripples as possible, convinced that the soldiers wouldn't enter my house. Faced with external danger, isn't this what most people tell themselves? Not me. It's the others. Don't see me. Don't come to me. Leave me alone. I'm innocent. I'm not like the others. The alluring illusion of invisibility!

The next day, they came through this very gate that I'm now entering, six of them, six fully armed Israeli soldiers without any sort of warrant. I was not immune. Of course not. The invasion was a real awakening. And they may well come again, and this time not only to enter and search but to do more. They could destroy the house. For the last fifty years they have been destroying thousands of Palestinian homes. By hoping against hope that I would be spared, I was choosing to forget that the policy is indiscriminate. I, a Palestinian, am always subject at any time to the whims of any Israeli soldier.

For fifty years I've been possessed by that feeling of insecurity whenever I come back to my house. Will this precariousness ever come to an end? Nothing lasts forever: not this occupation or these turbid murmurings of my heart. The day will surely come when I will be free of apprehension. Yet for now I needn't dwell in fear, for at long last I have found what I was searching for, my home, and no one can take it away from me.

Penny is still in her study. She has turned on the side lamp with the blue painted shade and it lights up the colourful, life-affirming painting by Samia Halaby that we had carefully chosen when we first came to live in this house. I can smell the

dish she is preparing for dinner. The table with the ceramic top in the courtyard is already set. I'll do my part for the meal and we'll sit outside under the lemon tree and eat.

I go to wash my hands before dinner and take a look at my face in the mirror. I find that I am able to smile back at the image I see.

I leave the bathroom and go out into the courtyard. On the stone wall are the mottled shadows of the branches of the lemon tree we planted in the middle that has now matured into full height and is laden with yellow fruits.

I look around me at our intimate surroundings and now call out to Penny, 'I'm home.'

Acknowledgements

Penny was, as always, my first and most treasured reader. Alex Baramki went through an early draft and made useful comments. My publisher, friend and editor, Andrew Franklin, provided important suggestions. Then the draft benefited from the able hands of my editor Penny Daniel. And as always the book was improved by the superb work of the copy editor, Lesley Levene. My friend the photographer Bassam Almohor provided the photographs. To all of them my sincere gratitude.

About the Author

Considered Palestine's leading writer, **Raja Shehadeh** is a writer, lawyer, and the founder of the pioneering Palestinian human rights organization Al-Haq. He is the author of several books including the 2008 Orwell Prize–winning *Palestinian Walks* as well as *Where the Line Is Drawn* (The New Press). He has written for the *New York Times*, the *New Yorker*, *Granta*, and other publications. He lives in Ramallah, Palestine.

Publishing in the Public Interest

Thank you for reading this book published by The New Press. The New Press is a nonprofit, public interest publisher. New Press books and authors play a crucial role in sparking conversations about the key political and social issues of our day.

We hope you enjoyed this book and that you will stay in touch with The New Press. Here are a few ways to stay up to date with our books, events, and the issues we cover:

- Sign up at www.thenewpress.com/subscribe to receive updates on New Press authors and issues and to be notified about local events
- Like us on Facebook: www.facebook.com/newpressbooks
- Follow us on Twitter: www.twitter.com/thenewpress

Please consider buying New Press books for yourself; for friends and family; or to donate to schools, libraries, community centers, prison libraries, and other organizations involved with the issues our authors write about.

The New Press is a 501(c)(3) nonprofit organization. You can also support our work with a tax-deductible gift by visiting www.thenewpress.com/donate.